Selling Your Business?

Get Prepared!

Revised, Second Edition

James Witham
&
Karen Laustsen

Selling Your Business? Get Prepared!

Revised, 2nd Edition

ISBN: 1541114574
ISBN-13: 978-1541114579

*This book is dedicated to the
hardworking men and women
who took risks to build their businesses.*

CONTENTS

Selling Your Business?
Get Prepared!

In the summer of 2001, we were working to complete an acquisition that was delayed because the seller was not getting requested information back to us in a timely manner. His books and records needed updating, he couldn't locate critical documents and he began second-guessing his decision to sell.

Then September 11th came. As a result of the ensuing mayhem, the closing was pushed back by several months, during which time the seller's business took a negative turn.

When the acquisition finally closed, it was at a lower price and with terms far less favorable to the seller.

Lesson: Since you can never anticipate and cannot control outside influences that may impact the completion of an acquisition, you should endeavor to never be the cause for a delay.

If you want to sell your business,

you need to be prepared!

1

LET'S GET STARTED

If you are contemplating selling your business, opening up your private company to an outsider's eyes can be intimidating. You may ask yourself: *"What will a buyer need to see?"* *"How should my documents be presented?"* *"Am I prepared to pass the due diligence scrutiny?"*

Most private business owners will sell a business only one time in their life. Most have not planned ahead. Most have no idea what is involved in the process. Most are totally unprepared.

We can boldly make these statements because we have experienced it first hand. Not just once or twice. But over and over again with companies we sought to acquire.

This book is designed to help you get prepared and to focus on the task of selling your business. Through it we will engage you to ascertain:

WHY? Why do you want to sell your business? Why would someone want to buy it?

WHO? Who are potential targets that would acquire your business? Who should you consult with? Who should you tell? Who needs to weigh in on the decision?

WHAT? What are you selling? What do you need to do to prepare? What documents are needed? What do you tell your employees? What do you provide to a prospective buyer? What is a buyer looking for and at? What is the business worth? What will you do afterwards?

WHEN? When is the best time to sell? When do you tell your employees, customers, vendors or investors? When do you sign a Letter of Intent? When do you sign a confidentiality/non-disclosure agreement? When do you need an appraisal?

WHERE? Where do you find a buyer? Where do you go for assistance? Where do you find the time to sell the business?

HOW? How much will it cost to sell? How do you determine an asking price? How should you present the company? How long will it take? How do you know if you should hire an intermediary? How do you prepare for a site visit? How do you handle meeting a prospective buyer?

Throughout this book you will see anecdotal stories of situations the authors have encountered when in various stages of making acquisitions. Some will illustrate pitfalls to avoid when selling your business. Others will reveal how potential buyers think or how deals get done.

At the end of most chapters you will find tasks related to the subject matter. To get the most out of this book, we suggest that you diligently complete these "assignments".

If you have a partner or major investor, we recommend doing this together. Should you decide to proceed on your own, please recognize that it is critical to know where you and your partner or majority shareholders may have conflicting thoughts *before* you are in discussions with a potential buyer.

There's a lot to do, so let's get started!

2

WHY PREPARE?

Making the decision to sell your company is often a highly emotional process. Most small business owners never plan for the day they will sell. Most are so myopically focused on operating and growing their business, that they do not have the time to, do not recognize the need for or do not know how to be prepared to sell.

It is particularly difficult to consider selling your business when you birthed it, nurtured it and guided it every step along the way. It is not easy to envision giving it up, walking away, moving on and leaving your "baby" in someone else's hands to raise.

For most entrepreneurs, it may be even more difficult to imagine staying with the company and working for someone else!

Being prepared to sell your business is vital for any business owner who is truly serious about selling. But it is also important for *all* business owners, even those not thinking of selling at this time.

In fact, the best time to get (and stay) prepared is before you ever need to or want to sell your business.

There are three primary reasons why it is important to always be prepared to sell your business: (1) Being prepared will reduce your stress throughout the selling process; (2) Being prepared will allow for a faster closing; (3) Being prepared will be helpful in the event you encounter one of the "What ifs" in life. What if you or a family member gets ill and you need to sell *now*? What if someone contacts you out of the blue wanting to buy your business? What if you die and your family wants to or needs to sell the business quickly?

As a business owner, there are three fundamental things that you must put in order when preparing to sell your business: *Yourself; Your Presentation;* and *Your Documentation.*

PREPARING YOURSELF - Preparing yourself for selling your company will help to protect against seller's remorse (unfortunately, a common occurrence) and will also provide for a smoother selling process and transition. This preparation includes taking into account personal psychological factors, financial factors and relationship factors.

In preparing yourself for selling your business, it is important to identify exactly why you are selling – which will be discussed in detail in chapter four of this book. Clearly identifying why you are selling will serve as the foundation for preparing yourself for the sale.

Next, you must discern what you would like to do afterwards. Stay on as an employee? Consult to the new owner? Retire? Start another business?

If you want to stay on as an employee, can you envision working for someone else? Can you really "give up the reins"? Will you be able to deal with not being the final decision maker? Will you be able to tolerate policy changes? Will you be able to handle having your employees seeing you answering to someone else? What if the buyer wants you to relocate?

If you would like to consult to the acquiring

company for a period of time, could you handle being marginally involved? Could you deal with your opinion not being taken into account?

If you just want to retire, can you afford it? Have you considered the benefits you receive from the company beyond your salary, such as bonuses, dividends, insurances, allowances and expenses? Do you know what you will do with the surplus of time you may garner? Can you handle the psychological implications?

If you want to start a new business, do you have a plan? Can you finance it? Is your family on board? Are you up to the task?

You also will need to consider the impact selling your business will have on relationships in your life. Is your spouse ready to have you home all the time? Or, if you work together, how much of your relationship revolves around the business? Will you have anything left to talk about?

What about relationships with a partner or employees? How will you react if they never call or do not have time for you? Will your employees think you bailed on them, be jealous or perhaps even think they deserve a portion of the proceeds of the sale?

What about your friends? Are most of your

friendships business related? Will you be able to handle it if these friendships dissolve? Will your friends be jealous that you sold your business?

Only you can prepare yourself. An honest inward evaluation and resolution of these questions will help you prepare yourself for selling your business.

PREPARING YOUR PRESENTATION - Everyone knows that the first impression is the lasting impression and that you only get one chance to make that first impression. Yet business owners, and in particular small business owners, seeking to sell their companies often do not provide potential buyers with an impressive initial perception.

More often than not, the initial presentation of the business is sub-par simply because the business owner is in unfamiliar territory and is not aware of how a potential buyer will view the presentation.

In later chapters, we will discuss how to prepare your business profile, the selling memorandum, the all-important "elevator pitch" and your facility, as well as the way to present your due diligence documentation to the prospective buyer.

Your presentation, both the written and verbal aspects, must come across as professional. And, clear concise communication is essential!

How you present yourself and your business to a potential buyer will set the tone for any negotiations that may take place. You must be sure your presentation is well prepared!

PREPARING YOUR DOCUMENTATION - As you move along through the acquisition process to the due diligence phase, you will be required to produce a significant volume of documentation to the prospective buyer. The operative word here is "significant".

Having as much of your documentation as possible prepared in advance will greatly reduce your stress throughout the process, and will also allow for a faster closing.

Most business owners anticipate that they will need to produce financial statements, but complete documentation production encompasses far more. You will need to expect that a buyer will want to also examine pretty much every document you have ever signed. And there is even more beyond that. It can be very demanding putting your documentation together, especially if you need to search for documents or need to reacquaint yourself with them, while at the same time running the business. Being prepared will make the process much easier with less tension.

The chapter titled "Preparing For Due Diligence" will address your documentation requirements in detail - not only what documents you need to be prepared to submit, but also the manner in which these documents should be organized and presented.

Being prepared to sell your business will be beneficial not only to you, but also to everyone else involved in the process. Once you find a potential buyer for your business, you want to be sure it closes as fast as possible and that you are never the reason for a delay.

In conclusion, remember that if someone is interested in potentially acquiring your business they are probably looking at other opportunities. The better prepared you are, the better the chance that *your* business will be the one selected.

You need to be prepared!

3

STEPS OF THE SELLING PROCESS

Upon completion of the tasks included in this book, you should be prepared to sell your business. In this chapter we will briefly explain the steps of the selling process. While there are no hard and fast rules, and each acquisition transaction is somewhat unique, there is a general pattern that is typically followed.

1. Attract a Buyer. Finding a potential buyer can be accomplished through various means. You can try to find a buyer through a broker or other intermediary, or on your own by advertising in trade journals and other appropriate periodicals, newspapers or websites, or by word of mouth. Depending on how discrete you wish to be about the sale will influence the method(s) you employ to find a buyer.

2. Send Business Profile to Potential Buyer. Your business profile will provide potential buyers with general non-confidential information designed to whet their appetite and make them desire additional information. A template from which you can develop your business profile is included at the end of chapter 13.

3. Sign Confidentiality Agreement. Prior to disseminating any additional information to a potential buyer, you should require the prospective buyer to sign a confidentiality agreement that includes non-disclosure and non-compete clauses. This agreement should be written by *your* lawyer. If for some reason you will be signing a prospective buyer's confidentiality agreement, it is important that it be fully reviewed and vetted by your attorney.

Some issues you should consider and discuss with your attorney regarding the confidentiality/non-disclosure agreement (NDA) include: (1) Agreements that do not contain a defined time frame are often more difficult to defend against if the other party does not honor the agreement. (2) Agreements often state that the only documents/information covered under the

NDA are those not publicly known or generally available, and which are marked "Confidential". It is extremely important that, if a similar clause is in an agreement, you are steadfast in marking *"Confidential"* on all your documents that do not contain publicly available information. This would include information provided in emails and any other written correspondence; (3) In the event that you verbally disclose confidential information, you should be diligent to follow up immediately with a written statement to the other party that the information you divulged in your discussion is protected under the NDA; (4) Consider including a non-compete clause in the NDA, so not only can the other party not disclose the information, they also cannot use it to compete against you. This is especially important if the prospective buyer is a competitor; (5) Consider including a clause that prohibits the other party from hiring any of your employees during the defined term, whether solicited or not.

It is important to remember that even after you have an NDA signed, you need to utilize discretion and not necessarily share *everything* about your operation, expecting it will be protected by the NDA. Since a lawsuit can be very expensive and perhaps difficult to

The Secret Sauce

The very first company we acquired had patented a chemical process that was included in our acquisition of select assets.

What was not revealed to us until after closing was that the inventor had altered the manufacturing process to enhance performance of the products without updating the patent.

Years later when the patent expired and competitors attempted to copy the patent, they could never get the product to work as well as ours.

Had he revealed this to us prior to closing, if the transaction did not close he would have been left in a potentially vulnerable position, especially if we had been competitors.

Lesson: Whether it is a secret recipe, computer code or your email list, keep your most protected proprietary information confidential until after the transaction closes.

prove damages, you should take things in stages on a "need to know" basis. There will be certain disclosures you will make following the signing of the NDA and before the Letter of Intent (LOI). After the LOI, and during the due diligence phase, you will need to disclose additional information. But often there is certain proprietary information that should not be shared until the deal is CLOSED.

This can be a balancing act. Remember, until the deal is closed, the business is still yours and you have a responsibility to yourself and any other owners or investors to protect it in the event the transaction does not close.

You need to be especially protective of information if you are selling to a competitor or other industry related party. Unscrupulous people have been known to purport they are interested in buying a company solely to learn more about a competitor's operation.

Think of it this way: If Kentucky Fried Chicken were being acquired, when would they reveal the secret recipe for the 11 herbs and spices? Not until the deal is closed!!

4. Meet with Prospective Buyer and Present Selling Memorandum. Unless there is a geographic constraint, it is recommended that you meet first with the potential buyer before providing them with your selling memorandum. Depending on your personal circumstances you may specifically *want* to meet at your place of business, or you may specifically *not* want to meet at your place of business.

During an in-person meeting, if you determine the prospect is a legitimate potential buyer and that you would like to go to the next level, you can present and review your selling memorandum with the prospect at this initial meeting.

If it is not possible to meet in person with the potential buyer at this point, it is important that you hold meaningful telephonic discussions with the prospect prior to disseminating your selling memorandum.

If you are not comfortable, feel that the buyer is not legitimate or for some other reason decide you would not want to proceed further, there is no reason to give out your selling memorandum. An outline containing the information you should include in your selling memorandum is included at the end of chapter 14.

5. Indication of Interest. At this point in the process, you may receive an "Indication of Interest" (IOI) or proposal from a prospective buyer. While most buyers and sellers will agree that a verbal indication of interest will suffice, some may prefer that it be in writing. The purpose of the IOI is exactly what it says…it is solely an indication that the person has an interest in going further and unless otherwise stated, is not in any way a legally binding document.

6. Initial Negotiations/Sign Letter of Intent. Once an interested party is isolated, initial negotiations will commence followed by the signing of a Letter of Intent (LOI). The LOI is a roadmap, normally written by the buyer's legal counsel and will provide an outline for the sale of the business based upon the initial negotiations, subject to the completion of due diligence. Think of it as an engagement agreement in which you are agreeing to marry the other party by a certain date, subject to certain terms and conditions.

The LOI typically will state what is being acquired (select assets, stock of corporation, etc.); the purchase price and terms; the anticipated closing date; and conditions of closing. Often a clause containing a breakup fee is included, along with certain restrictions on the seller's operation of the business, as well as restrictions on negotiating with other parties. It is imperative that your attorney reviews this document and that you negotiate salient points prior to signing.

While in one sense you are looking to enter into a

courtship, be aware that you are also in a chess match and under some circumstances negotiations will feel more like a boxing match.

Remember that anything you agree to in the LOI will be difficult for you to alter in the final agreement. However, it is important to note that the buyer will almost always want to make changes in the final agreement based upon information obtained in the due diligence phase. So be prepared for that!

In certain unique situations, sellers request a deposit or "earnest money" at the time of the signing of the LOI. This is ordinarily non-refundable and is applied against the purchase price at closing. However, take note that it may have to be returned if the due diligence process reveals material facts contrary to what had been disclosed in the selling memorandum or initial discussions.

Be aware that many buyers are not willing to put up earnest money, so if you plan to request it there must be a very compelling reason for a buyer to agree to it.

7. Commencement of due diligence. The due diligence process can be very stressful for sellers, particularly if they are not prepared. Upon completion of this book and the associated tasks at the end of most chapters, you should be well prepared for a smooth and speedy due diligence process!

A crucial issue to remember is that undisclosed liabilities are fraudulent, so disclose, disclose, disclose! It is better that the deal not close because you were honest, than to close and have you facing lawsuits over misrepresentations.

Keep in mind also that the buyer's findings during the due diligence process will almost always lead to more negotiating. Expect to be in negotiations all the way through to closing on price, structure, timing, employees, etc.

8. Final Purchase Agreement. The Final Purchase Agreement – whether in the form of a Stock Purchase Agreement, Asset Purchase Agreement or other similar format - is commonly written by the buyer's legal counsel in accordance with the terms and conditions laid out in the LOI. And do not forget, in almost all circumstances, you will need to be prepared for another round of negotiations based upon modifications the buyer will want to make following due diligence.

Be aware that in the final agreement, you will be required to make certain representations and warranties regarding various issues related to your business.

The most important thing to remember before

signing the final agreement is to be sure you have fully disclosed any potential liabilities and that your responses to the representations and warranties are complete, accurate and factual. And remember that until the closing, you continue to own the business.

9. Closing. Closing generally takes place shortly following the signing of the Final Purchase Agreement, and often based upon certain contingencies being satisfied. The documentation and/or contingencies required for closing will be included in the Purchase Agreement. It is only upon closing that you will receive payment from the buyer and that the purchaser owns the company.

4

WHY ARE YOU SELLING?

The first consideration when thinking of selling your business is to determine the *primary* reason you are selling. The reason for selling your business will fall into just two principal categories:

    1. You *want* to

    2. You *have* to

Let's first look at the reasons why people *want* to sell their business. The most common reasons people want to sell their business are:

- A desire to retire with no heir-apparent to take over

- Want to spend more time with family
- The acknowledgement that they cannot (or do not desire to) take the company to the "next level"
- The company has outgrown them
- A desire to diversify their assets
- They feel the timing is "right"
- They're burned out or bored with the business
- The business was inherited and the successor has no desire to operate the company

Generally speaking, business owners who fall into this category of *wanting* to sell their business have more flexibility and "staying power" to find the best deal for themselves. Without a pressing deadline or issue, they can be more selective of prospective buyers, more demanding regarding certain terms and conditions and can take a firmer stance with respect to the selling price.

Most business owners, particularly small business owners, however, fall into the second category of *having* to sell their business. The most common reasons people *have* to sell their business are:

- Health issues

- Divorce
- Dispute amongst partners
- Negative cash flow
- Sustained losses
- Debt obligation
- Business was inherited with significant tax issues
- Extenuating legal issues

Unfortunately, being in the position of *having* to sell a business often means the seller will be negotiating from a weaker vantage point and is more likely to have to settle for a less than optimal deal.

If you must sell your business, and need to do so quickly, you need to realize that you may not get as much for it as if you had time to continue searching for the most suitable buyer.

Having said that, you do not need to roll over and play dead, or be a proverbial deer in headlights! Remember, that even if you are desperate to sell, the prospective buyer does not necessarily need to know that.

While reasons such as negative cash flow will become readily apparent to the prospective buyer in the due diligence phase of the process, if it is your *main*

Under the Gun

A friend lost a lawsuit and as a condition of the final settlement, was given a short deadline in which to sell her business.

Without much time, and wanting to be sure she sold before the terms of the settlement became publicly known, she quickly and quietly contacted competitors in the area, solicited bids and commenced an auction for the sale of her business.

The closing was completed before the buyer realized she was "under the gun" to sell. Had they known, she possibly would have gotten less money for the business.

Lesson: No matter how desperate your situation may be when selling your company, never let a potential buyer know it!

reason for selling, they do not need to know that. And, there is no reason to disclose if you or a family member is ill or if you are going through a divorce. Always remember, **if they sense desperation they will haggle for a better deal.**

The most important first step in selling your business is to be totally honest with *yourself.*

If you do not *have to* sell, you should also consider how certain you are that you even *want* to sell. Seller's remorse is more likely to occur when a business owner has waffled on whether or not they really want to sell their business at a given point in time.

You should attempt to identify the triggers that might make you change your mind on your decision to sell. In your evaluation you should consider things such as: Receiving a large contract; signing up a considerable number of new clients; improvement in the company's financial condition; potentially beneficial regulatory changes; new strategic alliance opportunities, etc.

So in preparation for the task to follow, sit back and think: "Why am I considering selling my business? What are the pros and cons of doing so?" Be sure to take into consideration the perks you may be getting from the company, such as a car or car allowance or insurances you would have to pay for out-of-pocket after a sale.

In a later chapter we will develop your "elevator pitch" to allow you to concisely portray your reason(s) for selling to a prospective buyer. But for now, this exercise is solely for your benefit, to get you to focus on the real reason(s) you are selling your business.

You do not need to share this with anyone else unless you want to. *So if your primary reason for selling is because you are tired of working with your partner, say so!*

After careful thought and consideration, before proceeding to the next chapter, we recommend you complete the following task, writing your thoughts down in as much detail as possible.

I am considering selling my business because

☐ I **WANT** to

☐ I **HAVE** to

Main reason for selling:

_____

_____

_____

_____

_____

All other reasons for selling:

_____

_____

_____

_____

_____

_____

_____

_____

_____

_____

_____

_____

_____

List the pros and cons of selling (Use additional paper if necessary.)

Pros	Cons

On a scale of one to ten, how certain are you that you want to sell your business? _____

Under what circumstances would you possibly decide not to sell?

_____

_____

_____

_____

_____

_____

_____

5

WHAT ARE YOU SELLING?

The next important step in selling your business is to determine what you are selling. The simple response most people give is, "My business." Usually, it is a bit more complicated than that.

Most small business owners want to sell 100% of the stock of the corporation, including all assets and liabilities. Others may want to sell just a portion of the stock to an investor or strategic partner.

On the other hand, sometimes a business owner prefers to keep the corporation, and sell off select assets such as a division or subsidiary, a product or product line, a patent or other intellectual property. It is advisable to confer with your tax advisor regarding any potential tax implications of selling the stock versus selling the assets. This could have a considerable impact on the type of deal structure you would be willing to accept.

While you may prefer to sell the corporation, if a potential buyer just wanted to purchase certain assets what would you be willing to sell? It has been reported that 94% of all small businesses sold are asset sales only, so even if it is your desire to sell the stock of the corporation, you need to be prepared in the event an asset purchase is the only offer you receive.

In order to determine what you would be willing to sell, it is important to first identify your most valuable assets, recognizing that your intangible assets could hold considerable value. Under some circumstances, you could sell a significant asset for as much as or more than the company. For example, have you considered the potential value of your customer list, the number of unique monthly hits to your website or even your telephone number?

If you own the real estate that the business operates out of, do you want to sell that as well? Would you be willing to provide an option on the real estate to the buyer? Or would you prefer to retain ownership of the

And...what exactly are you selling?

An advertised acquisition target looked appealing and after an initial email communication with the seller we inquired about the asking price.

Upon hearing the number, which we felt was high, we followed up with a couple of standard questions, such as: "What is your corporate structure?" and "What are you selling"? (i.e. the corporation or assets)

It took the owner three weeks to finally let us know that she was a sole proprietor and did not have a handle at all on what she was selling.

Since she could not provide a clear understanding of what she was selling for such a high price, we walked away.

Lesson: If you advertise your business is for sale, know exactly what you are selling, and be prepared to communicate it clearly, both verbally and in writing, especially if your asking price does not match the readily perceived value of business.

property and obtain a long-term lease from the new owner of the business?

The next question is: How flexible are you? If a buyer only wants to purchase select assets, or does not wish to acquire the real estate, is that a deal breaker for you? Sometimes what you want to sell and what someone wants or is willing to buy are two very different things. In preparation for selling your business, it is important to identify to yourself what your limits are *before* you talk to the first prospect.

During this process it is also important to determine where you personally fit into the equation, particularly if you view the company as an extension of yourself. Do you want to stay with the company for a period of time? If so, for how long and in what capacity? How flexible are you on this? Will you find it difficult to work for someone else? Will you be able to adjust to someone else make the decisions – particularly those with which you may not agree? Would you be willing to relocate? If so, how far? Where would you be willing to go versus "no way am I going there"? Some people might view relocating to Alaska as an exciting adventure while others would view it as a punishment!

Flexibility

We found a small company for sale in Louisiana that manufactured a product line of interest to us. We did not want to purchase the corporation, nor did we want to buy the real estate - just specific assets.

The problem was that the assets we were interested in acquiring were being held as collateral in connection with an SBA loan.

We told the owner that if she paid off the loan, we would buy the assets we wanted for the same price she was originally asking for the corporation and the real estate.

Within four months she had sold the building and used the proceeds to satisfy the SBA loan. We closed on the deal within 60 days.

(Side note: Through the process of selling the building, she learned she loved selling real estate. She got her license and became a top broker in her area!)

Lesson: The more flexible you are, the greater the chance you will be successful in closing the sale. It is best to determine just how flexible you are before speaking with a prospective buyer.

If you really want to retire and move to a hammock by the ocean, what will you do if the buyer wants you to stay with the company? Conversely, if your desire is to remain with the company, what if a buyer does not want to include you as part of the acquisition? Is that a deal buster for you? Can you afford it financially? How about emotionally?

So, sit back and think… "What do I want to sell?"

Do you want to sell the stock of the corporation? Do you just want to sell select assets? Do you want to stay with the company? If real estate enters into the equation, do you want to keep it or sell it?

Now let's get ready for your task. In order to help put you in the correct frame of mind to determine what you are selling, it is recommended that you first determine the pros and cons for each decision you will need to make. Then, for each decision, determine your first choice and decide how flexible you are beyond that.

> *You may need to consult with your accountant and/or attorney to provide advice that will help you make these decisions.*

List the pros and cons of selling all or part of the *stock* of the corporation

Pros	Cons

List the pros and cons of selling *assets* only

Pros	Cons

List the pros and cons of selling the *real estate* (If applicable)

Pros	Cons

List the pros and cons of *staying* with the company

Pros	Cons

Now, identify what you want to sell and your level of flexibility

☐ I want to sell 100% of the stock of the corporation

    ☐ I'm flexible

    ☐ Not flexible

☐ I want to sell a portion of the corporation's stock

    ☐ I'm flexible

    ☐ Not flexible

☐ I want to sell certain assets only

    ☐ I'm flexible

    ☐ Not flexible

☐ I want to sell the real estate (if applicable)

    ☐ I'm flexible

    ☐ Not flexible

☐ I want to keep the real estate (if applicable)

    ☐ I'm flexible

    ☐ Not flexible

☐ I want to stay with the company

    ☐ I'm flexible

    ☐ Not flexible

☐ I do not want stay with the company

    ☐ I'm flexible

    ☐ Not flexible

Write down the driving forces behind each of these selections. If you are flexible, elaborate on just how flexible you are. If you only desire to sell certain assets, be sure to write down specifically what you want to sell, along with what you specifically want to keep.

_____

_____

_____

_____

_____

_____

_____

_____

_____

_____

_____

6

WHY WOULD SOMEONE BUY
YOUR BUSINESS?

When preparing to market your business to sell it, you will be more likely to target the right buyer if you have identified the reason(s) why someone would want to buy it. These reasons may not initially be evident.

If your business is profitable and has a positive cash flow, or if it operates in a growing or attractive industry or category, it is probably apparent why someone would want to acquire it. But what if it is not in a hot category or if it is barely surviving? Why would anyone want to buy it under those circumstances?

Operator Needed

Our company needed to purchase a highly sophisticated piece of laboratory equipment in order to perform clinical trials for submittal to the FDA.

The manufacturer of the equipment informed us it was critical that the person operating the device be highly proficient in order to ensure that the test results were not compromised.

We asked if they could recommend anyone in our area that we could hire and were directed to the owner of a small laboratory, which owned the same equipment.

After meeting with him, we purchased his company, through which we not only obtained our highly proficient operator, but also the laboratory equipment we needed!

Lesson: There are more reasons than you could ever imagine why someone would want to buy your business. Think outside the box!

Often entrepreneurs are so entrenched in operations, that they miss the big picture. Other times, they see only the proverbial *forest*, and not the trees!

So, step back and look at your company as if you were an outsider looking in. What do you see? What are ALL the potential reasons someone could have to want to buy your business or a part thereof? Why would a strategic buyer want to purchase your company?

Here are some thought provoking potential issues to consider. Depending on your industry or the nature of your business, some may not be applicable. Likewise, there will be numerous considerations specific to your unique circumstances not listed, so you'll need to evaluate what those considerations are that might apply to your particular situation.

- Are you a threat to a major competitor?
- Can you clearly communicate the differentiating factors of your business?
- Do you have a compelling competitive advantage?
- Do you operate out of a great location with a long-term lease?
- Do you have highly trained or specialized employees?

Medical Devices and Toys?

We were awaiting the release of the final ruling of a newly promulgated federal government regulation to spur demand for our medical device equipment. When the government delayed the enactment, we needed to find a way to increase revenues for our impatient public stockholders.

We came across a manufacturer of children's toys interested in being acquired. They had sustained rapid growth with moderately high revenues and a significant backlog of orders. But given the nature of the business, they had poor cash flow at certain times of year.

By acquiring the toy company, we were able to meet their cash flow needs while providing our stockholders with the increased revenues they desired – albeit from a very different source.

Shareholders and competitors, who only looked at the revenue numbers reported to the Securities and Exchange Commission without reading the full report to discover their source, marveled at the significant increase in our company's sales!

Lesson: Publicly traded companies can have very unique reasons to make an acquisition. It could make perfect sense to them, leaving others scratching their heads!

- Have you launched a new product line?
- Do you have an extensive client list or high level of unique monthly visitors to your website?
- Do you have a great reputation in the industry?
- Do you have a strong or exclusive relationship with certain customers?
- Do you have a strong or exclusive relationship with key vendors?
- Do you possess complex molds or tooling?
- Do you have regulatory approvals or licenses that may be difficult or take a long time to obtain?
- Do you have an "interrupting technology"?
- Do you have a strong patent, brand name or other intellectual property?
- Do you have a usable Net Operating Loss (NOL) carry forward? *(Must meet qualifications of Tax Reform Act of 1986. Check with your accountant.)*

Take into consideration that publicly traded companies or private equity groups often have very different strategic reasons for making acquisitions than do private companies, so be sure to take into account all considerations.

Now sit back and think about it... "WHY would someone want to buy my company?" Be thorough – including any and all possible reasons someone might have for buying your business, or any part thereof.

In going through this exercise, it is equally important to identify why someone would NOT want to acquire your company. Be brutally honest with yourself, looking at it from an outsider's perspective so that you can be prepared to overcome objections or position your offering around an issue that may be potentially troublesome.

Now, it is time to write it down!

List the TOP THREE reasons why someone would want to buy your business.

1._____

_____

_____

_____

2._____

_____

_____

_____

3._____

_____

_____

_____

Now write down all the other potential reasons why someone should consider buying your business.

_____

_____

_____

_____

_____

_____

_____

_____

_____

_____

_____

_____

List the primary reasons someone would *object* to buying your business.

_____

_____

_____

_____

_____

_____

_____

_____

_____

_____

_____

_____

_____

How would you overcome these objections?

_____

_____

_____

_____

_____

_____

_____

_____

_____

_____

_____

_____

_____

_____

_____

_____

_____

_____

_____

If you were a potential buyer – or were buying out your partner - why would *you* buy your company?

_____

_____

_____

_____

_____

_____

_____

_____

_____

_____

_____

_____

_____

_____

_____

_____

_____

_____

_____

7

WHEN SHOULD YOU SELL?

Determining when to sell your company requires analysis, strategy and the compass used most often by scores of entrepreneurs…"a gut feel"!

If you find yourself in a difficult position that is requiring you to sell the business, your simple answer to the question of when to sell may be "right now", or even, "yesterday". But remember, even if you are in a desperate situation, it is important to make sure you are as prepared as possible for the sale before listing it or engaging a broker or intermediary.

In some respects, determining when to sell your

All In Agreement Say "Aye"

We signed a letter of intent with the President and Chief Accounting Officer of an acquisition target and began the initial due diligence phase.

Shortly into the process, we met with the controlling shareholder, who abruptly announced that he had no intention of selling his stock.

The company's President was embarrassed and mortified. Although we were entitled to a breakup fee, we opted to just walk away.

Lesson: Before initiating the selling process, be sure you and any partners or majority stockholders are in agreement to sell. If you are not, it could not only be embarrassing, but could create a costly legal entanglement, as well.

business is not unlike making a decision to sell your house. You would analyze the home sale market in your area, consider what you would need to do to the house to prepare it for sale and strategize when would be the best time of year to list it.

Likewise, the analysis procedure for selling your business involves evaluating more than just your company. It also involves an analysis of the direction of the industry or business segment in which your business operates.

Some things to consider when analyzing the industry are:

- Is the industry growing, or on a decline?
- Are there new competitors?
- Are regulatory issues going into effect that could influence the industry in either a positive or negative way?
- What are the trends in the industry and how does your company fit within them?
- Is a consolidation movement taking place in the industry?
- Is the business seasonal?
- Are smaller businesses being squeezed out by larger corporations?

When analyzing your business, you should also determine what you need to do to prepare the company for sale, and how long it would take you complete those tasks. Among other things to consider are:

- Are your partners or majority stockholders in agreement?
- Do you need to get your financial books in order?
- Do you need to document your manufacturing procedures?
- Is your facility looking "tired"?
- Are you ready to launch a new product or marketing plan?
- Are there employee or operational issues you should address?
- Is there a deal you need to complete?
- Are you involved in, or facing potential litigation or other legal issues?

You also need to be sure to analyze considerations such as potential first rights of refusal you may have granted to another party; restrictions in a franchise, distribution, investor, partnership or other applicable agreements; pending contracts; and any other conditions that may affect the sale of the business. You should also consider who might need to approve the transaction, such as the Board of Directors, majority stockholders or partners, lenders or governmental agencies or, if applicable, a franchisor.

In determining the best time to sell your business, it is equally important to assess your personal situation and objectives, such as:

- Are you financially prepared to sell your business?
- Are you emotionally prepared to sell your business?
- Is your family on board?
- What will you do with your time?
- Would you want to stay with the company as a consultant or employee, if possible?
- Are you certain you want to sell your business?

Consider also these three red flags that often impact a potential buyer's decision to acquire a given business and what you may need to do, if possible, to buffer your business from them.

Red flag #1: Too narrow of a customer base or non-repeat business; Red flag #2: Overly dependent upon the owner; Red flag #3: Poor internal controls, accounting policies and/or procedures.

If you do not have to sell immediately, following this analysis, if applicable, you may want to consider addressing these "red flag" issues.

You might also want to attempt to increase the bottom line and value of your company by reigning in unnecessary costs while increasing sales and marketing efforts. You may wish to consider divesting of obsolete inventory, unused or under-used assets and even unproductive employees.

You may consider revisiting operating procedures and pricing policies as well as conducting a review of your vendors and suppliers to insure you are buying at the best prices and with the best terms.

If you are heavily involved in the day-to-day operations, but do not wish to stay with the company following the sale, it is also recommended that you begin delegating tasks to make the business less dependent upon you.

You should also take into consideration that your company generally has the greatest appeal to a potential buyer when sales are increasing and profit margins are strong. Unfortunately, many owners first consider selling their company when sales are flat or on a decline, or when profit margins are being squeezed.

So once again, let's get ready for your task. Sit back and think:

- What are the main considerations for determining the timing of the sale of your business?

- What are the considerations of the industry?

- What are the considerations of the company and its operations?

- What are your personal considerations? Do not forget to consider your personal financial position and potential tax implications of a sale.

- What is your "gut feel"?

You may need to consult with your accountant and/or attorney for advice that will assist you with this analysis.

List the considerations from the *Industry's Perspective* that could affect the timing of the sale of your business:

_____

_____

_____

_____

_____

_____

_____

_____

_____

_____

_____

_____

_____

_____

_____

_____

_____

_____

_____

_____

List the considerations from the *Company's Perspective* that could affect the timing of the sale of your business:

_____

_____

_____

_____

_____

_____

_____

_____

_____

_____

_____

_____

_____

_____

_____

_____

_____

_____

_____

List the considerations from your *Personal and Family Perspective* that could affect the timing of the sale of your business:

_____

_____

_____

_____

_____

_____

_____

_____

_____

_____

_____

_____

_____

_____

_____

_____

_____

_____

_____

_____

_____

Discuss any other miscellaneous influential considerations, including your "gut feel":

_____

_____

_____

_____

_____

_____

_____

_____

_____

_____

_____

_____

_____

_____

_____

_____

_____

_____

_____

_____

_____

Based upon this analysis, I believe the best time to target putting my company up for sale is _____, for the following reasons:

_____

_____

_____

_____

_____

_____

_____

_____

_____

_____

_____

_____

_____

_____

_____

_____

_____

_____

_____

_____

8

WHAT'S IT WORTH?

Often the most significant question a business owner has when wanting to sell his or her company is also the most difficult one to answer: "What is it worth?"

The bottom line is that your company is worth what someone is willing to pay for it at the time you want to sell it.

Particularly in stressful economic times, the "value" of the business does not necessarily equate to its worth or what someone is willing to pay. Conversely, we have all seen seemingly outlandish valuations placed on businesses with little to no revenue or profit!

Unrealistic Valuation

We looked to buy an Internet based company that had been operating as a non-profit. From our perspective, the only real "value" of the company was their outstanding domain name and the number of unique monthly visitors to the website.

Unfortunately, the owners felt the company was worth many times more than what we were willing to pay.

We walked away from the deal and shortly thereafter, a similar website was bought by a publicly traded company. Their publicly filed documents revealed that they based the purchase price on $1.00 per each monthly unique visitor to the site.

Applying that formula to the company we were looking to acquire, had they accepted our offer, we would have significantly overpaid for the company.

Lesson: If you seriously want to sell your business, you must be realistic about its value and worth.

So how do you arrive at an asking price that is not unrealistically high, which could drive potential buyers away? Conversely, you want to be sure not to set a asking price lower than what you could – and should – get for your business.

Unfortunately, far too often business owners believe the business is worth considerably more than it is – especially if they operate in an industry that previously had higher valuations than what would currently be considered acceptable. Owners often are offended at what they consider to be low offers, or feel cheated or have seller's remorse if they sell at what they believe was too low of a price.

Many entrepreneurs endeavor to inject into the value of their business the years of "sweat equity" they put into it. Unfortunately, there are very few buyers who will recognize that worth or put much, if any, credence in it.

In order to sell your company, particularly if you need to sell it in a timely manner, you must be realistic about the price for which you are willing to sell. For small businesses, if the company is cash flow positive, it is usually the easiest way for a potential buyer to value it. However, if your business is not generating positive cash flow and your balance sheet and profit

Consolidation Strategies and Valuation

A fragmented industry in which we were involved was going through a major consolidation, primarily spearheaded by one company.

This publicly traded corporation was acquiring industry related businesses so quickly that as one of the top executives told us, "We're just closing on these deals as fast as we can and will figure out what we're going to do with them later."

The first group of companies was acquired for an amount approximately equal to annual revenues. As competition increased with other companies making frenetic purchase offers, the acquisition prices rose to two times revenues and then quickly jumped to three times, with their last major acquisition topping a multiple of four times revenue.

Lesson: Do not just base your asking number on historical prices paid for competitors. If a roll up is occurring in your industry, the frenzy may be your best friend in getting a higher price. Conversely, if you missed the proverbial wave, do not hold out for the higher price. You might not get another chance to sell if the acquisition action is slowing down.

and loss statement are less than impressive, it becomes more difficult to determine what it is worth.

A key consideration is that the price someone is willing to pay is often driven by *why* they want to buy your company, and how many other companies are available that meet that need. If they are looking to take a competitor out of the market, the value to them might be "X" dollars; whereas if they're looking to increase distribution or enhance a product line, it may be a multiple of "X" that they would be willing to pay.

Another consideration in determining the worth of your business is who the potential buyer is. If much of your value is in non-tangible assets that would be accounted for as goodwill, a publicly traded company may value it differently than a privately held or foreign entity.

It is obvious that the financial condition of your business will be the first determining factor in arriving at a valuation. For example, if the company is about to go out of business, a true valuation would most likely be based upon liquidation value. If it were in a growth mode, it would most likely be given an investment valuation. But either way, there is a "value" that will translate into its worth and what someone may be willing to pay.

Often a company will sell for a "fair market" value. There are many ways to arrive at a fair market value of a given company, and the seller will forever wonder if the best one was used. There are a number of firms that will charge a considerable price to provide you with a fair market valuation of your company, but the issue with many of these appraisals is that they can be unreliable and unrealistic. Although most fair market valuations are determined by guidelines set forth by the IRS, there are often subjective items to evaluate, with different formulas that can be applied. The unfortunate bottom line is that if you had three different firms provide you with an appraisal, you would most probably get three very different valuations.

There are times when it may be necessary to obtain a third-party valuation, whether it is of the entire business or of a key asset, such as a patent. Patents are one of the more difficult valuations to perform. As one mergers and acquisitions executive said, "Valuing patents isn't rocket science. It's much more difficult!"

Remember, even if you hire an appraiser, you will still need to establish an asking price. If you are looking to sell quickly, you may want to list the business at a price lower than the appraised value. Conversely, if you want to leave some room for negotiating, you may want to price it higher.

Although you may ultimately end up determining that you need to retain a firm to provide an appraised value, there are actually several ways you can get a ballpark idea of the worth of your business on your own.

Consider the following:

- While this may be a difficult question to objectively answer, try it. What would *you* be willing to pay for your business? If you had a partner and you were buying out his or her half, what would you consider in determining the amount you would pay to be the sole owner?

- What have other companies in your industry recently sold for? How is your business similar? How is it different? Since there may be mitigating circumstances involved with a comparative business or the structure of a deal that you may not be aware of, be careful when comparing your business that you do not get locked in on a price based solely on a comparative sale.

If you know of any publicly traded companies in your industry that have recently made an acquisition, information about the transaction is frequently readily available. You can obtain highlights of the acquisition from a press release issued by the public company, or you can access the company's filings with the Securities and Exchange Commission at www.sec.gov. This information, which in some cases may include the actual purchase agreement filed as an exhibit, would be found in an 8-K filing, a quarterly filing on form 10-Q or the annual report on form 10-K. These filings may also include information regarding the valuation method used, as well as disclosure on the reason for the acquisition. This information could be beneficial to you in positioning your company's sale and determining its value.

There are a number of articles and financial calculators available on the Internet that can be utilized to help you determine a ballpark value of your business. Be aware that most of these web-based models do not account for the value of particular assets such as a patent or other goodwill, nor on the other hand calculate the negative value of certain liabilities such as warranties or threatened legal action. They also may not take into account a broad customer base with recurring revenue – a highly desirable quality for a company to have.

Thinking Outside The Box

Wanting to gain entry into a specific industry, we contacted the owner of a small company that had technology we were interested in acquiring.

Although he was interested in selling, he was leery about opening up his books to us.

Our CFO proposed that he show us the top page of the last five years of tax returns, and that we would pay him the average of revenues over the past five years for the specific assets we wanted.

He replied, "You would do that?" We closed the deal shortly thereafter under those exact terms!

Lesson: The value of your company is what someone is willing to pay. Deals can get done when the parties think outside the box.

Also unaccounted for in such valuation models may be the negative value of having a high customer concentration (over 25%) or high vendor concentration (over 40%).

If you decide to make use of an Internet based financial calculator, it is recommended that you proceed with caution and use the results solely as a tool in assisting you to determine your asking price.

Another consideration is that your CPA should be able to give you an indication of the value of your business based upon the book value (the difference between the total assets and total liabilities shown on the balance sheet) but be aware that he or she may not take specific industry issues into consideration, as well as other non-financial related issues including the reason a prospective buyer may desire to acquire it. Again, this valuation can be used as one tool which, when combined with others, should enable you to arrive at an asking price for your business.

It is also important to consider that it is not just the selling price, but also the structure of the deal that will influence a buyer. For example, if your company is priced right but you will only accept all cash upfront, you probably will have a more difficult time selling than if you were priced higher than an appraisal may support, but will finance the sale and risk taking a down payment of 40% or less.

Statistics have shown that the lower the down payment requirement the faster a deal will be done; however, it is not without risk! Very often the seller is not able to collect the balance due, particularly if the new owner ends up bankrupting the company, which unfortunately happens frequently with small businesses. In fact, it is so common for a seller to not collect the balance, that it has been said a seller should consider anything he or she collects beyond the down payment amount to be a gift!

And bear in mind that even if the sales agreement stipulates you will regain ownership in the event of a default, you may not be getting back much in value.

It is important to remember that valuations and multiples are just the starting point. Other factors to consider when structuring the deal and determining the asking price include:

1. The Consideration. Consideration is what the seller receives in return for the business. It can be in the form of cash, stock, seller financing or any combination of these. Any consideration other than cash should be valued in accordance with the risk associated therewith.

As a rule, sellers will only take stock issued by a publicly traded company. If the stock issued is not freely trading – which is often the situation unless the issuing company had previously registered shares with the Securities and Exchange Commission designated for future acquisitions, the number of shares issued typically would be based upon a discount to the current trading price in order to absorb the risk of market fluctuations. In some circumstances, the seller may negotiate for a "put" option against the stock, whereby if the trading price drops below a negotiated price when the shares are free to be sold, the acquiring company will be required to issue additional shares to make up for the shortfall.

Remember that you may have a tax advantage by taking stock in the buyer's company as consideration. Check with your tax advisor to see what these advantages may be and if they are applicable before you begin negotiations on receiving restricted stock.

2. Earn outs. Often buyers will agree to pay additional consideration predicated upon future performance of the company, usually based upon projections provided by the seller. While not necessarily included in the purchase price, an earn out will allow the seller to collect additional consideration if the company performs as forecasted.

It is important to note that most earn outs are never realized. Sometimes this is due to overly zealous projections by the seller, in which case the buyer averted risk. But it may also be due to poor execution of the business plan by the buyer, in which case the seller has lost out.

3. Liabilities. The reason most small business acquisitions are asset deals only is because buyers are reluctant to take on the responsibility for past liabilities, particularly those he or she may not know about! If a deal is structured in which any liabilities are transferred to the buyer, the amount and nature of these liabilities will determine whether or not a buyer will agree to assume them, and if so how it will impact the price they will pay for the business.

Liabilities that raise a red flag with buyers include unpaid taxes, under-funded retirement plans, potential lawsuits, warranties, certain unfulfilled contracts or sales orders and credit guarantees.

It is paramount to remember that even if the buyer assumes all liabilities, if you had personally guaranteed a loan or did not pay certain taxes, in the event the buyer defaults on those payments you will be held responsible! Check with your tax advisor to see how you could minimize your personal risk for past due taxes.

4. Adjustments. Buyers will always look to take adjustments for any areas in which they see potential risk. These areas may include things such as retention of key employees, continuing relationships with significant vendors or customers, fees associated with the cost of the acquisition and many other industry specific issues. Be prepared for a deal structure that may take such things into account.

Another matter you may need to address is what the value of the business is when *you* are the company's most valuable asset! If someone is looking to acquire your business for *your* personal expertise, they could view purchasing your company as "baggage" and will commonly offer you less than what you feel it is worth. If *you* are the most valuable asset your company has, you need to work extra hard to demonstrate the value of the company outside of yourself to a prospective buyer.

Determining the value of a business can be an art as well as a science. Since there is not any one particular way to establish the worth of your business, we recommend starting with the book value and applying any industry specific considerations as well as considerations specific to your business.

From there, you will need to determine if that value corresponds to what someone would be willing to pay, and where you should set your asking price.

So… sit back and think about the best way for you to determine the asking price for your business. Now, get ready to write some things down.

Note: It is very important to consult with a tax advisor on the tax implications of selling your business.

Depending on if your business is a corporation, partnership or proprietorship, and depending on how the sale is structured can make a very big difference in potential tax liability.

Be sure you know the ramifications of the structure of a deal **before** entering into any transaction, including a Letter of Intent, with a potential buyer.

(1) If you were buying your company, what would be the considerations you would use in determining what you would be willing to pay? How much would you consider paying?

_____

_____

_____

_____

_____

_____

_____

_____

_____

_____

_____

_____

_____

_____

_____

_____

_____

_____

_____

(2) Would you be able to base an asking price solely upon book value, cash flow, revenue or profit, or a multiple thereof? Why or why not?

_____

_____

_____

_____

_____

_____

_____

(3) Do you know the amount similar businesses in your industry and/or geographic area have recently sold for? Do you know what methodologies or formulas were used to determine the selling price, or the structure of the deal?

_____

_____

_____

_____

_____

_____

_____

_____

_____

_____

_____

_____

_____

_____

_____

_____

(4) Having previously determined why someone would want to acquire your company, how do these determinations weigh in on the value and/or the price you would ask for your business?

_____

_____

_____

_____

_____

_____

_____

_____

_____

_____

_____

_____

_____

(5) Do you anticipate you will need to hire a third-party to help determine an asking price? If so, why?

_____

_____

_____

_____

_____

_____

_____

_____

_____

_____

_____

_____

_____

_____

(6) If you believe you <u>do not</u> need a third-party to help determine an asking price, what is a price range you would consider? $_____ to $_____

(7) What is the absolute *lowest* selling price you would consider? $ _____   Would you take less for an all cash deal that closes quickly? ☐ Yes   ☐ No

_____

(8) What liabilities would you consider remaining liable for?

_____

_____

_____

_____

_____

_____

_____

_____

(9) What liabilities would you absolutely not consider remaining liable for?

_____

_____

_____

_____

_____

_____

_____

_____

_____

_____

(10) What type of deal structure would you *propose*? What would you be willing to *accept* and why? What are your "must haves" versus the "nice to haves" (All cash upfront; seller financing; earn-out; cash and stock; stock only etc.)? Be sure to take into account your determinations from chapter five of what you are selling (i.e.: assets only, real estate, etc.)

Deal structure you would propose:

_____

_____

_____

_____

_____

_____

_____

_____

_____

_____

_____

_____

_____

_____

Deal structure you would be willing to accept:

_____

_____

_____

_____

_____

_____

_____

_____

_____

_____

_____

_____

_____

_____

Other Thoughts and Considerations:

_____

_____

_____

_____

_____

_____

_____

9

THE COST OF SELLING
YOUR BUSINESS

Most business owners are not prepared for the costs associated with selling their business, both the "soft" costs and "hard" costs. When selling your business, you will probably find that you will have to spend money in order be successful; but, you want to be sure to spend it wisely and only where and when necessary.

Most often overlooked is the consideration of the *soft* cost of your time being spent away from the company's operations and the impact that it could have on revenues, profits and relationships with employees, vendors and customers. Considering that most companies take six months or more to sell, if at all, taking too much time away from the business to concentrate on selling it could have a long-term devastating affect. This is especially true if the business ultimately does not sell.

It is recommended that you develop a plan with a timetable in order to properly allocate the time you will need to devote to selling your business and to determine how you will handle both tasks effectively. Your level of involvement in day-to-day operations will most likely dictate the amount of time you will be able to set aside for the task of selling the business. Therefore, the more deeply involved you are, generally the longer it will take you to prepare the business for sale, find a buyer and have the transaction close.

Remember, that unless you are planning to stay on with the company, a potential buyer may be hesitant to move forward with an acquisition if it is obvious you are heavily involved with every decision and area of operations. So now may be a good time to start letting go and testing the capabilities of your key employees by delegating more tasks.

The other consideration is the *hard* cost of retaining professionals. You could, under some circumstances

A Costly Decision

When we made our first acquisition, we decided to hire a friend as our attorney. He was an outstanding lawyer, but had no acquisition experience.

The purchase agreement required us to pay a royalty on sales for a period of five years to the former owner who had invented the products.

Three years thereafter, we made an acquisition of an unrelated business that brought significant revenues into our company.

The owner/inventor from the initial acquisition claimed he was entitled to royalties on *all* revenue, whether or not it was derived from sales of the products we acquired from him.

Unfortunately, because the purchase agreement of that first acquisition was poorly worded, we ended up having to pay him royalties on sales of the unrelated company's products.

Lesson: Be sure to retain professionals with extensive experience in acquisitions in your company's size range and within your industry.

consider selling your business without hiring any professionals; however, in order to maximize the selling price and be sure you are protected legally and understand potential tax ramifications, you should consider retaining certain professional organizations or individuals to assist with the sale.

The professionals you may need to retain include:

- Attorney
- Accountant/auditor
- Appraiser
- Business broker or other intermediary

It is important that any professionals you hire are trustworthy and have experience with acquisition transactions. Here are some issues to consider when hiring these professionals:

Attorney

It is of utmost importance that your legal counsel be both reputable and heavily experienced in dealing with acquisition transactions. Prior to retaining a lawyer, it is strongly recommended that you interview not only the firm's managing partner (or "rainmaker") but also the lawyer that would be assigned to you. Be sure that it is a person with whom you feel comfortable working and who has the requisite background. It is important to ascertain that he or she is *personally* experienced in acquisition transactions in your company's size range and preferably in your industry, and not just that the firm they work for has such expertise.

It is also recommended that you verify your attorney's standing with the bar in the state(s) in which they are practicing. Most states have a website you can visit to easily learn if they have violations or at any time had been suspended. This is a more common occurrence than one would think, particularly with sole practitioners.

Be sure to know what the costs will be going forward through the completion (closing) of the sale. Those hourly rates can add up real fast!

While it may be tempting to hire your brother-in-law or old college roommate, if their expertise is in a different field of law, it could end up costing you more than what you would save.

When working with an attorney, while you want to be sure they vet the legal issues, we recommend that the business decisions and negotiations take place between you and the buyer – not between attorneys. There have been a lot of deals that have fallen apart because the attorney played the role of the entrepreneur. Let your lawyer counsel you on ideas for the structure of the deal or the ramifications and potential risks of a contentious issue, but in the end, be sure *you* are the one making the business decisions.

Accountant/auditor

In order to sell your business you will need to present financial statements to the prospective buyer. The more professionally prepared they are, the greater the potential of receiving an offer.

If you do not have a person in-house to prepare your financial statements, we recommend that you hire someone – preferably a CPA - to do so. You will need updated financial statements whether or not you will be hiring an auditor.

As with hiring a lawyer, be sure the accountant is a person with whom you feel comfortable working and who is reputable. You may want to consider utilizing a firm such as AccountTemps who will perform background checks on the individual(s) assigned to you.

Because there will be some buyers who will require that your company be audited before they would even consider a purchase, it is recommended that you retain the services of a registered public accounting firm to have your books and records audited, unless it is cost or time prohibitive.

When it comes to hiring an auditor, some business consultants will tell you that you need to hire one of the "Big Four" auditing firms. No, you do not! First of all, they are expensive and as a small company you will have a "junior's junior" assigned to your company. Speaking from personal experience, the inexperience of a low-ranking worker coupled with the corporate structure of the big firm will probably increase the time it takes to complete the audit, not to mention the cost. While the prestige of a large firm used to be synonymous with confidence, trust and reliance, remember that some of the largest auditing firms were implicated in the fraud charges levied upon large corporations, such as Arthur Anderson with Enron, and more recently Ernst & Young with Lehman Brothers.

Having said that, it is important that you hire a reputable firm. We would suggest selecting from the list of entities registered by the Public Company Accounting Oversight Board (www.pcaobus.org). Most of the firms listed also audit private companies and you will be assured of their credentials. Be sure to do your own further investigation on firms you select before interviewing them. One way to gauge whether or not they work in a timely fashion is to review the

SEC filings of public companies they audit to see if there is a pattern of untimely filings of 10-Q and 10-K reports. If there are one or two companies that are consistently late there is a chance it is due to internal issues of the reporting companies. However, if most of the companies have late filings, you must assume that the auditors are contributing to the tardiness.

It is very important to be sure you know up front what the complete charges will be for the audit before retaining the firm and how long it will take to complete it. And remember that the better prepared you are, the faster and smoother the process will be.

Appraiser

There are a slew of "experts" who can provide you with a valuation of your company. These experts can come in the form of an investment banker, CPA, business broker or a firm that specializes in appraising businesses.

As discussed previously in chapter eight regarding valuing your business, if you hired three different entities to provide you with an assessment of the worth of your business, you will likely receive three diverse valuations.

While it ordinarily is somewhat easy to provide an

estimate of the value of your business if solely relying upon book value, it becomes more difficult if there is a need to determine fair market value based upon a patent, trademark or other intangible assets. Although the opinions of various experts will differ in determining value, having an appraised value prepared by a reputable source could possibly add credibility to your asking price.

There are times when during the negotiation process there is a wide spread between what a buyer and seller feel is a fair market value, and they will utilize a third-party to provide the value of either the entire business or of a significant asset, such as a patent. The cost for obtaining a third-party valuation can be high and may not be worth the difference in the price for which you could sell. As a matter of caution, you should also consider that the valuation might come in lower than what you think the business is worth, and the seller would be armed with substantiation to pay you less.

If you ascertain that you need to hire a firm to provide a valuation, proceed with caution. There are many unscrupulous, uninformed or unworthy firms and individuals that will vie for your business.

As with retaining other professionals, it is imperative that you interview them, check references, and confirm that they not only are well experienced in providing valuations but that they also have experience in your particular industry or in the field for which you are hiring them. For example: If your primary reason for hiring the firm is to evaluate the worth of a patent, be sure the person or firm you retain is experienced in evaluating patents within your field. And be sure their expertise is in valuing businesses for the purpose of selling them, as opposed to valuing them for estate purposes.

Business Broker or Other Intermediary

One of the main considerations when selling your business is whether to hire a broker or other intermediary, or to sell it on your own. In fact, it is such a major consideration, the entire following chapter has been dedicated to this topic. While there may be some benefits in certain situations to engage an intermediary, it is important to recognize that they can be quite expensive and you need to fully evaluate if the cost is worth it. Sometimes the ten or more percent they charge can make a very big difference in what you walk away with in your pocket, especially if you are financing a portion of the sale and the broker is getting his full fee at closing.

There are certain things to take into consideration if you are leaning towards hiring an intermediary.

First and foremost, the broker must be someone you trust explicitly to work on your behalf. Whether you are using a business broker, M&A firm or investment banker, it is imperative that you interview them, check their references and verify their recent experience in your industry and with companies in your size range. Check with the Better Business Bureau and also with the International Business Brokers Association to verify the credentials of a broker and that there haven't been any complaints or lawsuits filed against them.

Take note that there are currently entities offering franchises and business opportunities for people desiring to be business brokers. Some of these folks may have only been in business a short time and have no acquisition experience. Be aware also, that some states require business brokers to be licensed. If that is the law in your state, be sure the broker you hire is properly licensed.

The cost of hiring a broker is typically 10% of the selling price for companies under $1,000,000, although reportedly, some charge as much as 15%. For acquisitions of $1,000,000 and more a sliding scale known as the "Lehman Formula" is commonly applied. The original Lehman Formula was 5% of the first million, 4% of the second million, 3% of the third million and 2% of the balance; however, this formula has been updated to now be known as the "Double Lehman", whereby the seller pays 10% of the first million; 8% of the second million, 6% of the third million and 4% of the balance. Some intermediaries may also propose a "modified Lehman" that fits in somewhere between the two.

If the value of your business exceeds $2,000,000, and you are considering hiring an intermediary, you may want to consider engaging an M&A firm familiar with larger transactions. If selling to a publicly traded company, some suggest utilizing an investment banker to represent you, especially if the buyer is represented by a banker. Be aware that many of these larger firms require significant upfront fees with monthly retainers in addition to a success fee upon closing a sale.

It is a standard practice that if your business is not sold during the time frame that you engaged the intermediary, you are still obligated to pay them if you sell the business within 18 to 24 months to anyone they introduced to you. Since "introduced" can be a loosely applied term, you should be sure that it is clearly defined. A broadly applied definition is anyone who signed a confidentiality agreement.

When hiring a broker, you should make every attempt to negotiate not having to pay them if you find the buyer on your own, even during the engagement period. It may be a difficult task to get them to agree to this; however, if they do not perform as anticipated and you find a buyer on your own, you probably would not be very happy paying them a fee if they did not render any services.

Other Considerations

There are always going to be other miscellaneous costs associated with selling your business. One of the biggest considerations is potential tax liability. It is recommended that you discuss tax ramifications with your accountant prior to putting your business up for sale.

Other considerations include: Costs required for "cleaning up" your facility; settling potential legal issues; preparing your sales memorandum; updating your website; updating your marketing materials, etc.

So, now it is time for you to evaluate the costs associated with selling *your* business.

Time Considerations

Based on the amount of time you spend running your business in comparison to your "free" time, what impact will your time needed to sell the business have on operations?

☐ No impact at all. I'm not involved in day-to day operations.

☐ Nominal impact. My staff handles most of the operations.

☐ Moderate impact. I should be able to find the time.

☐ Significant impact. My life revolves around the business.

What are the *top three* areas of your business that would be the most impacted by your diversion of time?

(1)_____

_____

(2)_____

_____

(3)_____

_____

_____

What time consuming tasks can you delegate to which employees, partners or consultants?

(1)_____ to
_____.

(2)_____ to
_____.

(3)_____ to
_____.

(4)_____ to
_____.

(5)_____ to
_____.

Based upon my involvement level in day-to-day operations and the impact my diversion of time could have on my business, I anticipate I will be able to dedicate _____ hours per week to the selling of the business.

Hiring Professionals

Evaluate and where possible identify the professionals you feel you will need to hire in connection with the sale of your business:

(1) Attorney: ☐ Yes ☐ No
Why or why not?

_____

_____

_____

_____

_____

_____

_____

Who? _____

Anticipated Cost: _____

(2) Accountant/CPA: ☐ Yes ☐ No
Why or why not?

_____

_____

_____

_____

_____

_____

_____

_____

Who? _____

Anticipated Cost: _____

(3) Auditor: ☐ Yes ☐ No

Why or why not?

_____

_____

_____

_____

_____

_____

Who? _____

Anticipated Cost: _____

(4) Appraiser: ☐ Yes ☐ No

Why or why not?

_____

_____

_____

_____

_____

_____

Who? _____

Anticipated Cost: _____

> **Since the next chapter is dedicated to the topic of hiring a broker, we recommend the following analysis for hiring a broker or intermediary be done following completion of that chapter.**

(5) Broker/Intermediary: ☐ Yes   ☐ No

Why or why not?

_____

_____

_____

_____

_____

_____

_____

Who? _____

Anticipated Cost: _____

_____

Any other thoughts and considerations related to the cost of selling your business:

_____

_____

_____

_____

_____

_____

_____

_____

_____

_____

_____

_____

_____

_____

_____

_____

Total anticipated cost to sell business:

$_____

10

SHOULD YOU HIRE A BROKER?

As previously discussed, there are several pros and cons associated with hiring a broker or other intermediary. Only you can evaluate whether or not you would be better off hiring a broker or selling your business on your own. Only you can assess if their fee of 10%, or more, is worth it to you.

Many business owners make the mistake of thinking that if they hire a broker, they will liberate themselves from being involved in the process.

Unfortunately, that is not true. Some might even say it ends up taking more of their time since they will need to educate the broker about their company and continually be available to field additional questions.

In order to properly assess whether or not hiring an intermediary is advantageous to you, it is important to be acquainted with the services that a broker or other intermediary can provide. Here are a few:

Provides Discretion

For some, the primary benefit of hiring a broker is that an intermediary can be more discrete in selling a business than can the owner. It is far easier for a broker to conceal from employees, investors/lenders, customers, competitors and vendors that you are selling your business. For example, an intermediary can call a competitor without revealing that they are calling on your behalf. They can also begin discussions with a potential buyer without anyone else being aware of it. So if confidentiality that your business is for sale is of utmost importance to you, you should consider hiring a competent broker.

Finds a Buyer

A good and experienced business broker or M&A professional should have access to and knowledge of a roster of potential buyers for companies in your industry and/or size range. At a minimum, they should know the best places to advertise your company. But the question to ask is, does he or she know any better than you? If discretion is not important to you, and if you have the time to dedicate to the process, you can probably advertise in the same places a broker would, and you may have the added benefit of being able to use word of mouth in your industry if you sell it yourself.

Generally speaking, the larger the business, the fewer prospective buyers and the greater potential need for an intermediary in order to find a buyer in a timely manner.

Depending on the industry and your company's particulars, a qualified intermediary may be able to solicit bids from a number of potential buyers who have received information about your company, and in essence hold an auction to sell it.

Helps Determine Value

There are some brokers or M&A professionals who will be able to provide you with a range of an asking price for your business, or even a full appraisal. Take note that buyers will often not consider an appraisal from the seller's broker as having been provided by an unrelated third-party. If you are looking for a broker to provide such assistance to you, it is important to ascertain that they are very familiar with your particular industry as well as any specific nuances of your business that should be taken into consideration.

Beware of brokers that may provide you with an unrealistically high valuation in order to obtain your listing. If one broker quotes a significantly higher value than others you have interviewed, they probably will not be able to sell it at that price.

Also consider that a broker may undervalue your business to get a quick sale so he/she can collect fees and move on. Unless a quick sale is equally important to you, be certain that the broker is providing a fair valuation.

Assists With Document Preparation

Since it is in the best interest of a broker that your company looks attractive to prospective buyers, an experienced business broker will provide or assist you in writing a business profile and/or selling memorandum to present to potential suitors. A few will also provide assistance with the due diligence process in order to facilitate a faster closing. Some may also provide guidance in evaluating a Letter of Intent, Confidentiality Agreement or Purchase

Agreement. It is strongly suggested that you be careful to not take any legal advice from a business broker unless he or she is also a lawyer with acquisition experience.

For the most part, by the time you complete this book and its tasks, you will already have a business profile and selling memorandum and will be well prepared for the due diligence process. If you have an attorney that will provide the legal documentation, you will not benefit much by hiring a broker to perform these tasks.

Helps With Negotiations

Some people thrive on the negotiation process, while others deplore it. If you do not like the process, or recognize you do not have a flair for it, a broker can help you negotiate with a potential buyer on the salient and potentially contentious points of the agreement.

A significant consideration is whether or not you plan to stay on with the company as either an employee or a consultant. The negotiation process can become highly emotionally charged, and sometimes downright ugly. Having a third party to negotiate the more contentious points will keep you at arm's length, making for a more pleasant relationship with the buyer going forward.

Another point to bear in mind is that a broker familiar with the process may be more likely to recognize when a buyer is being unreasonable, trying to take advantage of you or even being dishonest.

While the broker should be acting in your best interest, you need to be careful that he or she is not just looking to close the deal to make commissions and move on to the next project, and therefore not be negotiating in your best interest. Bear in mind that an inexperienced broker could actually stand in the way of negotiating a good deal.

If you are an experienced negotiator and have a good understanding of the process, if your company is small and the deal is not complex, you are probably better off negotiating directly with the buyer.

In the event you decide to hire an intermediary, here are some things you should know:

(1) Hire the right firm. Based upon the size of your business, you will need to determine if you should hire a business broker, an M&A firm or an investment banker to act as an intermediary, as discussed in the previous chapter. Thereafter, you need to be sure to select a firm that is familiar with your industry and one

---

that you completely trust. Since you will be spending a great deal of time with him or her, be sure to select someone with whom you would be comfortable working.

(2) Be prepared to spend the time required to familiarize him or her with your business. Being armed with a completed business profile and selling memorandum, combined with your updated, reviewed or audited financial statements, will greatly enhance the learning curve. (Expect that the broker may want to make changes to your business profile and selling memorandum, as they often want it to follow their own format.)

(3) Follow up with any of their requests in a timely manner. An intermediary will understand you are busy running the business, but if you show no sense of urgency, they will not either and will instead focus their time and efforts on other clients.

(4) Be sure to negotiate the best possible deal, including: (a) no upfront fee; (b) lowest possible commission rate; (c) non-exclusive; (d) no commission if *you* find the buyer; (e) commissions paid to them as you collect from the buyer, not all upfront at closing if you accept a pay-out over time.

(5) Be honest and upfront about any potential issues

that may arise. Do not put them in a position to learn about a problem from an employee, customer, vendor or investor – or worse yet, from the prospective buyer!

(6) Be clear about who they may have access to on your behalf – whether employees, customers, bankers, investors, etc. Overly zealous brokers can hurt you! If you do not want them interfacing with certain people, tell them upfront, or better yet, make it part of the agreement! Note that by restricting their access, they could use it as a reason why they could not sell your business.

(7) Watch out for scams. Some unscrupulous people will take your money and do no work. It is best to pay only upon success; however, most larger M&A firms or investment bankers will want upfront fees and/or monthly retainers. So be aware of potentially large upfront fees, and be certain to fully vet any firm that asks for upfront or even monthly fees. If there are monthly fees, be sure you have "outs" in the contract if you are not happy with their work.

(8) Some larger M&A firms or investment bankers will offer assistance to optimize the operations of your business or restructure it prior to introducing you to prospective buyers. Be aware that these services are usually not free. You need to determine whether or not

you believe these services to be necessary and to know upfront what it will cost in cash and also potentially in stock.

(9) Stay on them. Call or email frequently, especially if you are not hearing from them. Ask them what they are doing to find a buyer and be sure they are working diligently on your behalf.

So now it is time to sit back and determine if you should hire an intermediary to sell your business.

List the specific pros and cons you would personally have by hiring an intermediary:

Pros	Cons

☐ I need to retain an intermediary

☐ I do *not* need to retain an intermediary

☐ I'm not sure, because:

_____

_____

_____

_____

_____

_____

If you believe you need to retain an intermediary, select the category:

☐Business Broker   ☐M&A firm   ☐Investment Banker

Why?

_____

_____

_____

_____

_____

_____

_____

_____

What do you anticipate will be the cost of hiring an intermediary? $_____

Before continuing, please go back to the previous chapter to include this anticipated cost of hiring an intermediary to the projected total cost of selling your business.

11

FINDING A BUYER

"He who has a thing to sell and goes and shouts it in a well, is not as apt to get the dollars as he who climbs a tree and hollers." You need to make it known that your business is for sale!

The methods you use to find a buyer will be dependent upon a number of considerations. First of all, if you do not want your employees, customers or vendors to know you are selling your company it may be more difficult to find a buyer on your own and, as previously discussed, you may be best served by hiring a broker.

You never know where a buyer for your business

may come from. In almost every acquisition we have done, the seller would have *never* targeted us.

But having said that, it is important to establish a profile of who you think could be a potential buyer.

Are there any companies in your industry – whether a competitor, customer or vendor – who could potentially be interested in acquiring your business? If you operate a franchise, is there a fellow franchisee that may be interested in expansion? Would you consider selling to a key employee, friend or relative?

It may help you to focus in on who potential buyers may be by taking into consideration the exercise previously completed in chapter four on why someone would want to acquire your business.

Next, you need to target those you have deemed to be potential buyers. If you believe a private equity group could be interested in acquiring your business, you may want to consider making a presentation at an investment meeting.

If you believe a potential buyer is a competitor, you might want to advertise in a trade magazine. Remember, if you need to be discrete, you should consider setting up a different email address or cell phone number to which an interested party may respond.

Another option to consider is an ESOP (Employee Share Ownership Plan). If you believe this may be a good alternative, it is important to retain a reputable firm to set the plan up. This can be very costly, and it is suggested that you fully understand the benefits and risks associated with ESOPs.

Once you have decided to sell your business, you will need to create as much exposure of your company as possible, across as wide a spectrum of areas as possible. Be sure that everyone in your industry knows who you are, even if you are a small player. Issue press releases of pertinent matters; sign up to be a speaker at the next trade show; launch a creative product or service promotion.

A real estate broker will tell you they never know if it is the sign on the lawn, an open house or the listing in the local paper or Internet site that brings in the buyer. And it is the same thing for selling your business. You never know which avenue will produce the buyer. Since it cannot be predetermined, the more avenues you simultaneously pursue, the greater the chance of selling your business.

If you decide to try to sell without an intermediary, you will need to consider advertising in trade magazines, numerous website listings and directly

"I Won't Sell To You"

We stumbled across a company with a novel technology that we were interested in acquiring and building a new business unit around.

The owners all enthusiastically met with us, one of which included the inventor. Our due diligence and negotiations over several weeks were proceeding very smoothly until the inventor suddenly announced, "I won't sell to you."

He had unilaterally decided that he did not want to sell to a publicly traded company. Although the deal could have been completed with the other owners who held a majority of the company, without the inventor on board we were not interested in proceeding with the acquisition.

Lesson: If there is anyone you would not want to sell you business to, identify who it may be and do not waste their time or yours engaging in discussions or negotiations.

contacting targeted potential buyers. Remember that even if you are selling on your own, you can maintain some level of discretion by having a close friend or relative call a potential buyer on your behalf without initially revealing who you are.

In your quest to find a buyer, it is important to identify if there is anyone you would NOT want to sell your business to. Sometimes inventors will not want to sell their invention to a company that is not committed to developing the product and bringing it to market. They want to be sure their technology would not just be "put on the shelf."

Some people do not want to sell to competitors or to publicly traded companies. Some will not sell to a foreign corporation, or to a party who will move the business out of state, while others will not sell to an entity that is not committed to retaining their employees.

And others want to sell only to a new owner who they believe will preserve their legacy.

So, sit back and think. How will I find a buyer for my business? Who do I believe is the right buyer? Once again, it is time to write some things down.

Would you consider an Employee Share Ownership Plan (ESOP)?　　☐ Yes　☐ No　☐ Unsure

Will you be hiring a broker or other intermediary?
☐ Yes　☐ No　☐ Unsure

List any competitors you believe may be potential buyers.

_____

_____

_____

_____

_____

_____

_____

List any vendors you believe may be potential buyers.

_____

_____

_____

_____

_____

_____

_____

_____

List any customers you believe may be potential buyers.

_____

_____

_____

_____

_____

_____

_____

_____

List any other persons or entities you believe may be potential buyers.

_____

_____

_____

_____

_____

_____

_____

_____

_____

_____

Identify anyone that you would *not* want to sell your business to, whether a generic group such as a foreign corporation, publicly traded entity, competitor, etc., or a specific person or entity, and why. Also indicate whether or not you would be flexible in this determination.

I prefer *not* to sell my business to:

1._____because

_____

_____

_____

_____

_____

_____

☐ I am flexible   ☐ I am not flexible

2._____because

_____

_____

_____

_____

_____

_____

_____

_____

☐ I am flexible   ☐ I am not flexible

3._____because

_____

_____

_____

_____

_____

_____

☐ I am flexible   ☐ I am not flexible

(Use a separate sheet of paper to identify any others.)

_____

Identify business or trade magazines where you would consider listing your business for sale.

_____

_____

_____

_____

_____

_____

Identify websites where you would consider listing your business for sale.

_____

_____

_____

_____

_____

_____

Identify any other venues where you can advertise or otherwise make known that your business is for sale.

_____

_____

_____

_____

_____

_____

12

YOUR EMPLOYEES

For many business owners, one of the principal concerns when selling is the impact it will have on their employees. A significant consideration is when to tell which employees of an impending sale.

Informing employees that the business is for sale often makes them feel insecure about their future. Will the new buyer wish to retain them? Would they want to work for the new owner? What changes will the new owner make in the operation of the business?

Sometimes employees will take it personally that you are considering a sale. Some will become jealous that you will be "cashing out", and perhaps even believe they are entitled to a portion of the proceeds.

Some employees will become less productive; some may form a surly attitude; others will immediately begin a job search to see what opportunities may exist for them.

Since, unfortunately, most businesses do not sell in a timely manner, if at all, telling employees too soon that you are selling – or even considering selling – could end up harming you. It is therefore recommended that you only tell employees that you are selling on a "need to know" basis, and only at the last possible moment that they need to know.

Expect that some may feel slighted for not having been told sooner, but remember that you need to do what is best for you.

Obviously, if you believe that an employee or group of employees is a potential buyer, you will need to inform them of your decision to sell. However, even then, it is recommended that you not make any disclosure until such time that you are prepared and positioned to put it on the market. Telling them prematurely while you are putting things together could end up placing undue pressure upon yourself.

The next issue you will face as it relates to your employees is the extent to which you will go to protect

Employee Loyalty #1

While preparing to close on the purchase of a competitor, the president and largest shareholder directed us to issue a percentage of the stock he would be receiving in our public company to his loyal employees, with the largest amount going to one specific key employee.

All the employees, including the former president, stayed with the company after the acquisition was completed.

Shortly after closing, that key employee contacted us to "tattle" on the former owner with a tirade of disparaging comments, and quit shortly thereafter, taking the several thousand shares of stock with her.

Lesson: Usually an employee's loyalty is solely to your signature on their paycheck – not to you! Be certain they worth going out on the limb for.

them in the event of a sale.

Some business owners are of the mindset that employees are just that - employees. They did not take the risks associated with starting and running the company. They never went without a paycheck and never had a sleepless night trying to figure out how to finance expansion. As a result, they tend to not take the employees into consideration when negotiating and structuring a deal.

Other business owners feel compelled to take care of the employees that helped them build the business. Perhaps they worked for less pay or without benefits to help launch the company, or played a critical role in the growth or development of the company. As a result, the seller will often endeavor to include protection for these employees in the final deal.

There are some business counselors who will advise that a business owner is morally and ethically bound to ensuring the continued employment of their workers after a sales, even if it means getting less of a deal

Others tell business owners that they have an obligation to give employees time off to look for work during the transition period and to provide letters of recommendation. But unless the buyer had stated that he does not intend to keep these employees, such

Employee Loyalty #2

A friend recently sold her business. During the negotiation process, she went to great lengths to ensure that her loyal employees, many of whom had been with her for several years and whom she considered to be friends, would be taken care of after the sale.

As the weeks went by after the closing, she was devastated that not one of those "loyal" employees called her to say thank you, or to even just say hello and see how she was doing.

Lesson: While you might be friendly with your employees, under most circumstances, they are not your friends. When your business relationship ends, more often than not, so does your "friendship".

actions would potentially be a violation of provisions of the Letter of Intent and/or Purchase Agreement.

Some further counsel that the seller should provide or extend employment agreements to employees it wishes to protect in a sale of a company. But if the buyer is not interested in retaining these employees, this action could hurt the seller by creating a liability for the new owner that he or she may not wish to assume. Remember also that from the perspective of the employees, if the employment agreement contains a non-compete clause – as many do – in the event they do not like working for the new owner and want to quit, they may be precluded from finding a comparable replacement job.

How you decide to approach this issue is entirely up to you and you should not feel shamed into protecting employees at your own expense if you do not want to.

However, you should be careful to take into consideration your specific situation and that of the acquiring company. Issues that will influence this decision can include: Whether or not you will be staying with the company; whether or not you have been active in the business or been an absentee owner; if there are highly technical and/or key employees whose loss would have an impact on the buyer's future

A Right or Wrong Decision?

Due to health issues a friend needed to sell his business. He received two offers: One from a large company that would pay him cash up front but not retain any employees; the other from a minority partner who would pay him less for the business with a small down-payment and monthly payouts, but who would keep all the employees.

Considering how much he had complained about the poor attitudes of many on his staff, we were surprised when he sold to the minority partner solely because the employees would not lose their jobs.

As time went on the new owner lost clients and the monthly payments were often late. Despite outsiders questioning his judgment, this friend maintains he made the right decision to take less money in order to protect the jobs of the employees.

Lesson: Do not let outsiders influence your decision. If you feel morally obligated to protect the jobs of your employees, then you should do it. But be sure it is your own decision, or you may end up with seller's remorse.

success; or, if the buyer will be moving the company to a different geographical region.

In order to protect yourself from making an emotional decision as the sale process gets nearer to closing and as employees begin to learn about the sale, it is a good idea to evaluate your employees now to determine from your prospective how you would prefer they be treated in the sale. Think of why you would tell a prospective buyer that a given key employee or group of employees should be retained.

In your evaluation, identify if your assessment is to do what is best for the employee, for the buyer/company or for you.

Now, write it down. (Use additional paper if necessary.)

(1) Employee _____

    Position_____

Should be retained because:

_____

_____

_____

_____

_____

_____

_____

_____

(2) Employee _____

    Position_____

Should be retained because:

_____

_____

_____

_____

_____

_____

_____

_____

_____

(3) Employee _____

     Position_____

Should be retained because

_____

_____

_____

_____

_____

_____

_____

_____

(4) Employee _____

     Position_____

Should be retained because

_____

_____

_____

_____

_____

_____

_____

_____

(5) Employee _____

    Position_____

Should be retained because

_____

_____

_____

_____

_____

_____

_____

_____

(6) Employee _____

    Position_____

Should be retained because

_____

_____

_____

_____

_____

_____

_____

_____

_____

13

PREPARING YOUR
BUSINESS PROFILE

Imagine you are sitting in your office and the phone rings. The caller says, "I'm interested in buying your company. Send me some information." What would you send? How long would it take you to put it together? What impression would that first communiqué make?

If you have ever looked at buying a house, the first thing you request is an information sheet describing the real estate. These flyers offer a snapshot view of the property and usually contain a cleverly written paragraph that makes you want to go to the next step and arrange a viewing.

In order to be prepared for prospective buyers' inquiries, whether solicited or not, the same type of basic information sheet or "business profile" should be put together in advance. While it is understandable that a business owner would not have a prepared business profile if approached unsolicited, it is inexcusable to not have one if the owner is soliciting the sale of the business.

Even just the exercise of putting this information together in a written format will force you to have a more focused view of your company. After all, if you do not have an accurate picture of what your business is, you will never be able to convey it to a prospective buyer. You may find that you will need to update or tweak your business profile from time to time, but the basic information should remain constant.

It cannot be impressed upon you enough how important it is to be able to quickly respond to a potential buyer's request for information. There are many reasons why this is vital. A timely response will give the impression that you are organized and on top of things, which reflects on how well the potential buyer will perceive you have operated the company.

Turned Off

We responded to an ad for a small business for sale, requesting information about the company. The response, which came several days later, said information would be sent both electronically and via mail. A week passed and we received nothing.

We inquired again. Finally, some questions were answered, others ignored and we still did not receive the promised documents. When we got the information weeks later, it was presented in an incredibly unprofessional and incomplete manner.

Although interested in the business, we were turned off from pursuing it further, fearing the due diligence process would be a laborious undertaking.

Lesson: Be prepared to respond quickly and in a professional manner to a potential buyer, especially if you placed an ad or reached out to a potential buyer via another method.

Receiving a well-presented business profile in a timely manner will also make the prospective buyer anticipate that, if they end up having a desire to pursue the acquisition, you would be easy to work with and that there would be a smooth due diligence process.

Additionally, they may lose interest if it takes too long to get even the initial basic information to them. And, if they are looking at a number of potential acquisition candidates, you want to be sure they do not make a decision to acquire a different company while you are still putting your information together.

The most important thing to remember when preparing your business profile and subsequent selling memorandum is to be honest. In today's day-and-age where people have access to a plethora of information at their fingertips via the Internet, it is incredibly easy for a potential buyer to research you and your business.

And trust me, they check! If they have reason to believe you are not being honest in your initial communication with them, they will not have confidence that they could rely on any future information, and will probably not pursue the acquisition.

There are many templates available outlining the information you should initially provide to a prospective buyer. Since every company is as individual as the person running it, there is no one template that would fit every situation. Do not feel compelled to fit your company into a mold that is inappropriate. You can use the format provided at the end of this section, or any another one you may prefer, but always remember, *do not i*nclude any information that you deem to be confidential. If you are initially looking to hide your identity, you may not want to even include the name of the company!

It is recommended that your business profile present a range rather than exact figures for revenue, profit, cash flow and asking price. You will, of course be required to provide precise numbers at a future date if you and the prospect agree to move to the next level, and after a Confidentiality Agreement has been signed.

In addition to your business profile, if applicable, you may wish to send a prospective buyer your product information sheets or other marketing materials, relevant recent press releases or additional information that will highlight your company. The information you provide should be enough to whet a potential acquirer's appetite, but not enough to satisfy. Enough to just make them hungry for more!

How you send the information to the prospective

buyer also requires important consideration, with options being emailing an electronic file or sending hard copies. Bear in mind that an electronic file is very easy for the recipient to forward, which can be a positive or a negative depending on how discrete you want to be about the sale. If you send your profile electronically *always* send it as a PDF file in a format that does not allow changes to be made to it.

If you choose to send hardcopies, we recommend using an eye-catching envelope such as FedEx, Express Mail, or Priority Mail. Note that the recipient could perceive from an overnight shipment that you are desperate to sell, so 2nd day or Priority Mail may be more appropriate. Regular first class "snail-mail" should be avoided unless you are sending it in addition to an emailed electronic file.

Before starting, we suggest you do an Internet search on your company, its products or services and yourself. Your first step should be your company's website. Verify that it is up to date and make any necessary changes. You do not want to direct a potential buyer to your site, only to have to explain that you no longer provide a certain product or service!

Most people doing research on both you and your company will go to one – maybe two – search engines

A Tangled Web

An ad in the Wall Street Journal for a company for sale piqued our interest. In a brief initial conversation with the owner, he recommended we view his website.

The site was in obvious need of being updated. Numerous links did not work and in subsequent conversations with the owner we learned that a product highlighted on the site that was of significant interest, was not included in the sale.

Through a quick Internet search we found the company had an "F" rating with the Better Business Bureau, there were numerous consumer complaints and competitors offered significantly better pricing. The owner was seemingly surprised when we mentioned this to him, and had no explanations.

Lesson: Be sure you know what a potential buyer will see when they research you and your company. Change what you can, and be prepared to have an answer for the things you cannot.

and not go beyond the first five pages. We recommend searching the name of your company and its products or services, as well as yourself and other owners or key employees. Be sure to use two or more search engines, and go to the first TEN pages of each to ensure you do not miss anything. Have disgruntled employees posted disparaging things about you or the company? Have dissatisfied customers written complaints? Did the vendor you were feuding with voice his opinion about you on a blog or YouTube video?

Do not be alarmed if you come across information that is inaccurate, false or misleading. Most buyers know that not everything they read on the Internet is true, but if they have seen something that is questionable, they may make inquiries about it, so you should be prepared to address it at the appropriate time.

If confronted, be careful not to come across as being overly defensive, as it could lead to the potential buyer thinking that there may be some truth to it. ("Me thinkest thou doth protest too much" ~ *William Shakespeare. Hamlet.*)

You may consider compiling a list of inaccuracies you come across, and where possible attempt to have them corrected. For example, information contained on Hoovers and Corporation Wiki is often inaccurate or incomplete. You should be able to contact them and similar type entities to have such information removed or updated.

Another suggestion to consider is a service such as Reputation.com, which can help you control what people find when they perform an Internet search.

So now it is time to put together your business profile. As previously mentioned, the following template is just one proposed format. Your profile and its format should accurately reflect the look and feel of your company. Remember to keep it brief! One page is recommended – not more than two!

> *Before distributing your Business Profile, it is recommended that you have it reviewed by your legal counsel.*

BUSINESS PROFILE TEMPLATE

Company Name: Contact Person:

Address:

Telephone: Website:

Company Name	Legal name of entity and D/B/A if applicable. If appropriate, include any other names you may currently or formerly been known as. If you do not wish to disclose your identity at this time, simply say, "To be Provided" and eliminate the information from the top portion of this form.
Type of Entity	"C" Corp; "S" Corp; LLC; LLP; Sole Proprietor;, etc. If there are divisions or subsidiaries, include that information here.
State of Incorporation	State in which you are incorporated
Date of Incorporation	Date of incorporation. If operations started significantly after that date, make mention of that here
States authorized to do business in	List all states and jurisdictions in which you are authorized to do business. Delete section if you only operate in state of incorporation
Ownership	Number of owners and percentage of ownership of largest owners. (There is no need to mention owners by name at this time.)
Business Description	Insert a brief statement of what your business does including the industry in which it operates (i.e.: Pizza franchise; Manufacturer of widgets, etc.) and the geographical areas serviced (i.e.: Nationwide, Southeast, etc.)
Location(s)	Describe your location(s) including square footage and time left on lease.
Number of Employees	Insert number of employees. Specify the number of full time and part time employees.
Annual Revenues	Insert a range of annual revenue for the most recently completed year. If current year is trending differently, make note of that here.
Cash Flow	Insert cash flow for the most recently completed year. If not cash flow positive, consider eliminating this section.
Annual Profit	If profitable, insert a range of profit for the most recently completed year

INSERT YOUR "SELLING STATEMENT" to concisely communicate what you are selling and why someone should buy your company.

Briefly explain differentiating factors, competitive advantage, mention of proprietary or intellectual property, significant barriers to entry, appropriate business trends (i.e.: "sustained year-over-year growth"; or, "recently completed R&D for a new product launch"; or, "high gross profit margins" etc).

Include a brief statement of why you are selling.

Asking Price: $ (Insert price range)

14

PREPARING YOUR
SELLING MEMORANDUM

While creating a selling memorandum, sometimes called a sales memorandum, is not a requirement for selling your business, since many prospective buyers will desire to see one, it is suggested that you have one prepared. Producing such a document can make it easier for a potential buyer to determine if they would like to pursue the acquisition without having to needlessly take up much of your time, or theirs.

Your task is to create a document that will present your company in the best light. You will need to present informative facts (even the negative ones!) while making the reader feel a sense of excitement about the business. You need to be "selling" your business while being totally upfront and honest, and not misleading.

It is important to recognize that anything you say in the selling memorandum that is not accurate will most likely be vetted out during the due diligence process. So do not set yourself up for, at a minimum, an embarrassing situation by not being truthful.

The memorandum should be completely informative, yet concise. Some business owners make the mistake of thinking "more is better" and create an overly verbose document that doesn't get read.

Rarely will someone sit down and read an entire sales memorandum cover-to-cover. So it is best to produce a document that will correspond with the manner in which most prospective buyers will examine it:

Step 1: The Visual Interpretation. Does the finished product look professional? Does it engage the recipient to make them want to read it? Is it so thick they toss it aside for when they'll have more time to look at it? Is it so sparse they presume it must not be comprehensive enough?

Step 2: The Flip Through. Are there headings, charts, tables, graphs or appropriate illustrations or photos that provide a snapshot of the business? Is it laid out in a logical manner? Bear in mind that the financials are usually the first section to which the reader will flip.

Step 3: The Scan. Does the Table of Contents look informative and interesting? Does the first paragraph provide enough information to connect with the readers and make them want to read further? Are the Introduction and Summary engaging?

Step 4: The Perusal. When examined in detail will it hold the reader's attention? Is it easy to read? Is it free of glaring spelling and grammatical errors? Is the information complete? Is it consistent with that on your website? Does it justify your asking price? Does it make them want to pick up the phone and call you before someone else discovers this "gem"?

The details required in the selling memorandum are typically predicated upon the nature of the business and the size of the deal. If your business is a small retail shop, your memorandum will not need to be as detailed as if your business is a manufacturing company with proprietary and/or patented processes selling for several million dollars.

For smaller deals, a comprehensive business profile along with professionally prepared financial statements will often suffice in lieu of a selling memorandum; whereas very large deals are likely to have a selling memorandum that compares in form and substance to that of an investment prospectus.

Since your selling memorandum should have a professional and polished look, you may consider engaging someone such as a graphic artist to put the final touches on the document if you sense it does not have the right look and feel. And once again, remember that while it is a selling document and you want to tout your business, be certain that you are not overly optimistic in your presentation, particularly if you will be including projections.

Although it is not a legally binding document, since anything in the memorandum that is false or even slightly misleading could create liability for you, we recommend that you have this document reviewed by both your accountant and your attorney prior to distributing it to anyone, including an intermediary.

Being that confidentiality is paramount in selling your business it is crucial that you not distribute the selling memorandum to anyone who has not signed a confidentiality agreement. It is recommended further that you use discretion and not give it out to any party that you know you would not be interested in selling to, or who for whatever reason, you do not believe to be a serious potential buyer.

Although you will have signed a confidentiality agreement with anyone you hand it out to, there is a very good chance your selling memorandum will also be viewed by others that have not done so. Therefore, it is recommended that you be careful not to disclose information that could damage your company if the memorandum got into the wrong hands, particularly if the prospective buyer is a competitor.

We recommend delivering a hardcopy of the selling memorandum to prospective buyers, especially if the document contains a considerable amount of confidential information. Whenever possible, it is a good idea to personally present the memorandum to the prospective buyer when meeting with him or her.

Until you have signed a Letter of Intent, it is recommend that you not send any sensitive information via email, and even then, be cautious. When documents are sent via email, it becomes much easier for the recipient to forward the document to others, and impossible for you to control who views it. You would be astounded at some of the documents that we have received fifth and sixth hand via email from unsuspecting originators.

If you are leaning towards engaging an intermediary you will find that they will most likely require you to have a selling memorandum. Even though they will probably make changes to whatever document you put together, having such a document prepared will make it easier for them to be brought up to speed on your company upon their engagement, and to more easily produce a selling memorandum in the format they prefer.

Remember that this document is going to heavily weigh in on what the prospective buyer's impression is of your business. So be sure to allot the appropriate time to craft the document. It will always take much longer to do than you think! Since you may find yourself thinking of what to say or how to phrase a particular section at odd times – like when in the shower or driving - keep a notepad or voice recording device handy!

If writing is absolutely not your forte, you may wish to outline or bullet-point the key points of the manuscript and have someone else compose the memorandum for you.

Be sure to carefully proof read and edit the

document several times, and if possible have a third party scrutinize it before it is finalized and disseminated.

Following is a suggested outline for you to follow when putting your selling memorandum together. Depending on the nature of your business, certain sections may not apply and conversely there may be certain nuances to your business or industry that should be added.

Remember: It is very important that any projections you share include a disclaimer that such projections should not be relied upon in making a decision to purchase the company. Please consult with your attorney.

SELLING MEMORANDUM OUTLINE

1) Introduction and Summary (Executive Summary)

   a) Brief overview of the company

      i)   What you do

      ii) How long in business

      iii) Highlights of milestones achieved

      iv) Description of significant agreements, joint ventures, etc.

      v)   Brief description of the industry

      vi) Brief description of your products and services

      vii) Brief description of what you are selling

      viii) Brief description of why you are selling

   b) Financial highlights

      i)   Revenue

      ii) Profit

      iii) Cash flow

2) Description of the Company

   a) When incorporated and where

   b) Form of company (S Corp, C Corp, LLC)

   c) Ownership

d) Location(s)

e) Brief description of your products or services

f) Intellectual property

g) Competitive advantages

h) Strengths and weaknesses

3) Industry

   a) Description of the industry including trends, major competitors, profile of customers, barriers to entry

   b) Description of regulatory issue affecting the industry

   c) Description of your niche in the industry

4) Products or Services

   a) Detailed description of your products or services

   b) Discussion of percentage of sales of each product or product line

   c) Description of patents or other intellectual property

   d) Describe future products or services

   e) Benefits of your products or services in comparison to competitors

5) Customers

   a) Description of the target customers you sell to or service (Do not name customers)

   b) Geographical area(s) in which customers are located

   c) Disclose if there are any customers that represent more than 5% of your total revenue

6) Sales and Marketing

   a) Description of sales and distribution channels

   b) Advertising and marketing efforts *(Do not include proprietary strategies and other sensitive information)*

      i) Discussion of advertising and marketing efforts that were successful

      ii) Discussion of future opportunities that may be beneficial to company's growth

7) Organization and Operations

   a) Staff

      i) Organizational chart

      ii) Number of full time employees

      iii) Number of part time employees

      iv) Description of any key positions and discussion of reliance on any particular employee(s), if applicable

v) Description of organized labor, if applicable

vi) Discussion of employee longevity, turnover, significant issues

vii) Breakdown of employees by location, if more than one

b) Operations

i) Description of your operations

ii) Description of non-confidential operating procedures

8) Real Estate

a) Number of locations

b) Description of property(ies)

i) Type of facility (retail store front, warehouse, office etc.)

ii) Square feet

iii) Leased or owned (Disclose if property is owned by a director, office or stockholder and leased to the business.)

iv) Terms of lease

v) Age and condition of property

vi) Fair market value of owned property if included in the offering

9) Equipment

   a) Description of equipment utilized in the business

   b) List of equipment by location including age, condition and value

   c) Discussion of additional or replacement equipment that may be needed

10) Financial Information

   a) Financial Overview Discussion

      i) Current Revenues and trends

      ii) Current Profit/loss and trends

      iii) Cash flow

      iv) Discretionary and non-recurring expenses

      v) Significant Assets – Tangible and Intangible

      vi) Long and short-term debt

      vii) Tax liabilities

11) Future Plans

   a) Three to five year goals/projections

   b) Discussion of basis of these projections

   c) Effect of government regulation on future of the business

   d) Effect of industry trends on future business

e) Effect of R&D, new products etc. on future of the business

f) Resources required to achieve goals

12) Legal Issues

a) Disclosure of current law suits

b) Disclosure of pending or threatened legal action

c) Disclosure of regulatory deficiencies

13) Offering and Price

a) Description of what you are selling

b) Asking price

c) Terms

d) Basis of asking price

14) Summary

a) Summarization of the business

b) Summarization of offering

c) Selling statement – Why the reader should buy your business

15) Appendix/Exhibits

a) Product literature

b) Patents and other intellectual property

c) Applicable photographs, diagrams, illustrations

d) Financial Statements including applicable footnotes

    i) 2 to 3 years annual statements, preferably audited

    ii) Current year broken down by quarter

15

PREPARING FOR DUE DILIGENCE

There is nothing that will delay an acquisition from closing more than a prolonged due diligence process. It cannot be stressed enough that the better prepared you are for the due diligence process the easier, faster and less stressful it will be.

Since there are so many issues that will be out of your control when it comes to determining the timing of the closing of a deal, it is best that you do all you can to make due diligence a swift and smooth process for the buyer and never be the source of a delay.

Due diligence can at times make you feel almost like you are being violated. If you understand and look at it from the buyer's perspective, it may make it easier to get through the process. The purpose of due diligence is to allow the buyer to verify what he or she is buying and confirm that the condition of the company is what it is purported to be. This can make some sellers feel as if their honesty and trustworthiness are being questioned and will be offended by it.

The fact is that "yes", your honesty and trustworthiness *are* in fact being questioned, and unfortunately with good reason. There are many documented examples at every level of unscrupulous sellers and, as a result, the buyer needs to confirm that you are not one of them!

Buyers are well aware of many documented situations where, even after extensive due diligence by large companies, significant post-closing issues have arisen. So as difficult as it may be, do not take the scrutiny personally.

The due diligence process is customarily a two pronged process. The first is production of documents and the second is an interview/discussion with the seller. It is important to recognize that any information provided in these discussions will be cross-referenced with the documentation provided, so it is important to be consistent.

Who Owns the Company?

Getting ready to close on the sale of a Texas company, we received a list of the shareholders and their respective percentages of ownership.

While preparing the closing documents, an "updated list" was emailed to us, with the explanation that an employee had reminded the company's president that he and other employees had been promised ownership in the company.

The new list adjusted the percentage of ownership of the original stockholders to accommodate the added employees and we readied the closing documents accordingly.

At closing, the largest original stockholder refused to sign, stating she did not agree to have her ownership percentage reduced and had never been consulted regarding the redistribution. The closing was delayed for several weeks while the shareholders argued amongst themselves and the acquisition almost did not close.

Lesson: Be sure your corporate documents are updated and correct. And remember that a verbal agreement is as legally binding as a written agreement.

The potential buyer will most likely present you with a list of items he or she will need in order to complete due diligence. An example of such a list is included at the end of this chapter. The list you receive will probably look similar to this, but may be customized based upon on the nature of your business and the industry in which it operates.

A basic consideration is that the prospective buyer will want to examine pretty much every document you have ever signed, so be prepared for that!

The due diligence list you will receive can look quite intimidating and time consuming, particularly if it comes from a publicly traded company or private equity firm. The better prepared you are, the less intimidating it will be. It is also important to realize that many items on the list may not be applicable to you.

Below we will highlight the fundamental items you should review, update if needed and have ready for the due diligence process. We recommend assembling both hard copies and electronic files of the due diligence documentation and be sure it is presented in an easy to access format.

Electronic files should be indexed and categorized in appropriate folders. You may find that a prospective buyer or their intermediary will set up a due diligence "electronic deal room" on the Internet for sharing due diligence files.

Well-labeled files or a sectioned notebook work well for production of hardcopies. (We personally prefer the notebook!) We recommend making three identical sets: One for the prospective buyer, one for the auditor or other potential third-party, and one exact copy for yourself. Be sure to update your notebook with any additional documents that you provide throughout the due diligence process.

For extremely voluminous documents, most buyers will agree to view these items in your office to avoid the time and expense of copying or scanning. If applicable, be sure these documents have been segregated and are easily accessible.

Financial Statements. First and foremost will be to have your financial records up to date. If you have not kept your records current, and if you do not have anyone in-house to do so, it is recommended you hire an outside firm or consultant to assist you in putting these statements together. As previously discussed, companies such as AccountTemps can provide you with a qualified and vetted individual to prepare the financial statements. Keep in mind that most potential

Misrepresentations

We closed on the acquisition of a company in which we agreed to make monthly payments on bank debts that had been personally guaranteed by the former owners.

Within a few months it became apparent that much of the information provided to us by the sellers and attested to in reps and warranties, was grossly inflated and inaccurate.

Our remedy was simple! We stopped making the payments to the bank. Consequently, the bank pursued the former owners under the provisions of the personal guarantees!

Lesson#1: Be honest. You never know how or when the truth will come out, and when it does, it will never be a good situation.

Lesson#2: If you have personal guarantees on loans, leases or other encumbrances, if the buyer will be assuming the debt, wherever possible, negotiate to have those debts paid off at closing.

buyers will want to see three to five years of financials.

Small businesses are often encouraged to present "recast" financial statements that show net income without the owner's compensation and other discretionary nonrecurring expenses. If you decide to present your financials in such a manner we strongly suggest that you clearly communicate this to the potential buyer right from the start. You do not want the buyer to learn this during due diligence.

It is important to note that some companies will not consider an acquisition without having audited financial statements to review. If you have audited financial statements it could very possibly attract a greater number and/or higher-quality potential buyers. Having audited financial statements would also help to close the deal faster since buyers will likely rely upon an auditor's report to satisfy a portion of their financial analysis.

If a publicly traded company is acquiring your business, your financial statements will have to be audited and filed with the Securities and Exchange Commission within 45 days following the closing. Given this limited time frame to complete the audit, the acquiring company will want to ensure that your books and records are in sufficient condition to be audited before the closing takes place. Having your financial statements audited ahead of time may make you a more attractive potential candidate to be acquired by a publicly traded company.

If your company has never been audited by an independent auditing firm, this can also be an intimidating and stressful process. The better organized you are the easier and less stressful it will be.

Schedules. In addition to the financial statements you should, at a minimum, be prepared to provide schedules of fixed assets, current inventory, obsolete inventory, UCC filings, long term and short-term debt, current backlog, accounts payable and receivable aging statements.

Articles of Incorporation/Organization; Bylaws. If you are like most small business operators, you probably haven't looked at your corporate formation documents since the business was started. Whether you are a C Corp, an S Corp, an LLC or an LLP, it is very important that you review these documents and verify that you are in compliance with them and with any applicable state requirements. If there are any issues that need to be addressed, we recommend that you contact your legal counsel to ensure you have filed any required reports, paid all fees, filed required

Know Your Agreements

As a public company, we had announced the signing of the Letter of Intent with a target company, and shareholders were anticipating the announcement of the closing of the acquisition.

With due diligence nearly completed, we were awaiting a copy of an agreement that had been executed with a distributor.

Finally receiving the distribution agreement, we quickly reviewed it and to our dismay discovered it contained a clause providing the distributor with a First Right of Refusal to purchase the company we were acquiring! The owners of the company had completely forgotten that clause was in the agreement.

Now, dealing from a position of weakness, we had to negotiate with the distributor in order to close the acquisition. This negotiation took several weeks and resulted in the sellers of the company getting less when the deal finally closed.

Lesson: Be sure to review all of your agreements and know what is in them!

amendments to original articles, etc. This is a very important step since prior to closing the acquisition, you will need to present a Good Standing Certificate from the state in which you are incorporated. And you certainly do not want anything as simple as this to hold up the closing!!

Corporate Minute Book. Depending on the type of corporation and the state in which you are incorporated you may need to verify that your corporate minute book is up to date. If you are not in compliance consult with your legal counsel. We recommend that you never backdate minutes.

Stock Ledger. Even if your intention is to only sell assets and not the stock of your company, it is still important that your stock ledger accurately reflects the ownership of the company. If there are any issuances or cancellations that need to be made, be sure that these transactions are completed before the due diligence process commences.

Tax Returns. Be certain that you are current in all filings with the IRS. Buyers will probably want to see three to five years of filed tax returns. NOTE: If your social security number is shown on a tax filing, we recommend redacting it prior to providing a copy of the return to a potential buyer.

Permits and Licenses. Verify that any permits or licenses required for your operations are in place and current. You do not want non-compliance to be the reason closing is delayed since it is very simple to be proactive. You should also have a schedule of any certifications or approvals, the name of the governing body and applicable expiration dates.

Contracts and Agreements. Review *every line* of *every section* of *every contract* and agreement you have signed. Be sure there are no clauses that will impact your ability to sell your business, such as a first right of refusal.

You must also verify that the contracts are assignable. If not, in the event that the value of that contract is important or significant to the business, you will need to assess the risk of going to the other party and requesting an addendum. Generally, this is only needed if you are just selling the assets; however, some contracts will cancel if there is a change in ownership, so be sure to know what contracts you have signed that may be impacted by such a clause.

An assessment of your contracts may help you decide if you want to sell the stock of the company or just the assets, or could make a buyer who only wanted to purchase assets, be required to buy the stock of the

It's Taxing!

#1 A business we were acquiring was unresponsive to our request for the previous three years' tax returns. After numerous requests over several weeks, the owner said he had "just found them" in the desk of his former comptroller – and they had not been filed!

#2 Having signed a Letter of Intent, we began due diligence on a company organized as an LLC. Upon comparing revenues and profits reported to the IRS to the annual reports given to LLC members and then to the financial statements provided to us, there were significant discrepancies.

#3 Prior to even meeting with or signing a Letter of Intent with a targeted acquisition, the owner emailed copies of the company's tax returns. Due to the structure of the company, his personal social security number was included on the returns.

Lessons: Be sure your tax returns have been properly filed and that all information provided is consistent and accurate. If your social security number is included on the return, be sure to redact it before sending it to a prospective buyer.

company. For example, let's say you have a retail store that has operated out of the same great location for 20 years and that moving to a new site could impact revenues. If the lease is not transferable to a new entity, the new owner may not be able to effectively negotiate a lease with the landlord if he is only buying the assets.

If there are any key agreements that have or are ready to expire, if they are a critical component of what you are offering to a prospective buyer, now is probably the time to negotiate an extension. Note, in most cases you do not need to disclose that you are considering a sale of your company. Conversely, be careful not to extend a contract that could be considered a liability for a potential buyer. For example, extending a lease could be problematic for a buyer who would want to move the business to a different location.

It is also important to verify that both you and the other parties are in compliance with the provisions of the agreements. If not, if you can bring yourself into compliance without excessive cost or time, do so. If for whatever reason it is not possible, it is important to acknowledge and when appropriate disclose this information to the prospective buyer.

Assignment

We identified a competitor as an acquisition target where the owner only wanted to sell select assets.

Upon commencing due diligence and reviewing the company's agreements we learned that, unbeknownst to the owner, a contract with the federal government was not assignable to any other entity.

Given the significance of that contract, we informed the owner we would have to acquire the stock of the company. Although the deal got done, it was not under the terms and structure the seller anticipated.

Lesson: Knowing what is in your contracts and agreements can help you properly position your company for sale.

Remember also, that a verbal agreement is as equally binding as a written agreement. Verbal agreements will also need to be disclosed to the acquiring party.

Insurance Policies. Insurance policies are another set of documents that often have either never been read, or haven't been looked at since the day you signed them. We recommend that you review each one and verify that they are all up to date. It is also important to review these policies in connection with any agreements you have signed that may require you to maintain a certain level of insurance. Be sure you are in compliance with any such matters.

Leases or Real Estate Deeds. For any properties rented or owned, you will need to provide copies of leases or real estate deeds. You will also need a schedule and copies of any equipment and vehicle leases.

Customer Information. Buyers will typically want to see a schedule of your top 10-15 customers including two-year revenue from each with a notation of any customers representing more than 5-10% of your revenue. Be prepared to discuss the status and trends of relationships with these customers, as well as potential growth with each. (Note: If the prospective buyer is a competitor, you may want to redact the names of the customers when producing this information.)

Vendors. Buyers will need to gain an in-depth understanding of your suppliers, so you should be prepared with a schedule of major vendors, with a notation of any that are sole source providers, or any with whom you may have an exclusive agreement. Be prepared to discuss the relationships you have with your vendors and suppliers as well as your sourcing policies.

Competitors. In order to fully assess your business, a potential buyer will need to understand the competition and will usually request a schedule of primary competitors.

Be prepared to discuss the competitive landscape, including your position in the market in comparison to competitors, and your competitive advantage, whether it be price, product features, service, location etc.

Domain Name Registrations and Web Hosting Agreements. It is important that you provide information related to your domain name registration and web hosting agreements. Be sure your domain name registration and web hosting are not about to expire. If they are close to expiration, you should

Full Disclosure

As an expansion of our product line, we engaged in the pursuit of acquiring a manufacturer of a specialized laser.

The final purchase agreement had been signed containing the standard representations and warranties, and prior to closing, we had begun moving the manufacturing equipment and inventory into our facility.

When one of our employees learned of our pending acquisition, he began inquiring about it and informed us that an acquaintance of his had filed a patent infringement lawsuit against the company we were *thisclose* to owning!

We immediately unwound the deal with demand for payment of our costs.

Lesson: Withholding pertinent information is fraudulent. Provide full disclosure and let the buyer determine if a given issue is a "show-stopper" for him or her.

renew them for at least one year. At the appropriate time you will need to provide passwords, which we recommend be done at closing.

Product Information. A prospective buyer will probably want to learn as much about your product line (or service offerings) as possible. Remember that although you will have signed a non-disclosure agreement, until the acquisition closes you could be vulnerable if you share certain specific trade secrets and the deal does not close. If there is any information you wish to withhold, be sure the prospective buyer knows that you will be providing more detailed information following closing.

You should be prepared to include product descriptions and an analysis of revenues by product category, profit margins, analysis of life cycle of each product, targeted customers, warranty information and any product liability issues.

Also be ready to provide information on any new products about to be launched or in research and development, along with the status of time and cost to bring these products to market.

Sales and Distribution Information. A buyer interested in purchasing your business for your sales team will be particularly interested in information related to sales and distribution. Be prepared to provide a list of sales personnel, manufacturer's representatives and/or distributors, along with analysis of the percentage of sales generated by each entity for the past two years and compensation paid. Be prepared to discuss the selling cycle as well as objections faced when selling your products or services.

Employees. In addition to any Employment Agreements, be prepared to provide an organizational chart with job descriptions, as well as bios for key personnel, payroll records and a schedule of accrued vacation and sick days. Review each employees' files to ensure they are up to date and in full compliance with regulatory issues as well as company policy.

You will also need to provide a copy of the company's employee handbook, description of all employee benefits programs (including 401K or other retirement plan) and documents related to worker's compensation claims history, unemployment claims history, and any employee grievances including harassment, wrongful termination or discrimination.

Marketing. Most buyers will be interested in learning what marketing approaches you have pursued, and which have proven to be most successful. Be prepared to provide a copy of your marketing plan

Too Anxious To Close

We were proceeding with due diligence on a company operating in an industry in which we had no prior experience. A portion of our due diligence included an exploration and analysis of the industry, which caused the process to take a bit longer than usual. The seller was becoming increasingly agitated with all the questions we were asking about the industry as well as with the amount of time it was taking to close the transaction.

The pressure he was putting on us to close the deal made us suspicious, which resulted in us proceeding more cautiously. Fortunately, our intuition was correct. Between the time we signed the final agreement and the scheduled closing date, his company was raided by the FBI.

Lesson: Do not be overly anxious or put persistent pressure on the buyer to complete the deal. They will become suspicious and even if you have nothing to hide, it could slow down – not speed up – the process.

NOTE: The company was innocent of all assertions and allegations; however, given unrelated issues, we did not proceed with the acquisition.

along with an analysis of marketing and advertising programs launched and their level of success.

Legal Issues. It is imperative that you provide full disclosure on any legal issues you are currently facing or have had in the past. Be prepared to provide documentation related to any current, pending or threatened litigation as well as any judgments awarded or settlement agreements. Also include any information related to previous or potential health, environmental or employee safety violations.

Intellectual Property. Since the value of any intellectual property is conventionally an issue for a buyer, be sure you have all the documentation they will need to assess these items. Be prepared to provide patent, trademark or copyright documents including any letters of opinion from counsel, as well as any legal action that may have been filed against any of them. You should also provide a description of technical "know how" (or a statement that this information will be fully disclosed at closing) and policies pertaining to protection of trade secrets.

Operations. Buyers will be interested in learning what makes your business "tick". Be prepared to provide your operations manual along with any other internal documentation pertinent to the operation of the

All On Board

We signed a Letter of Intent with the majority shareholders to acquire their company. Unbeknownst to us, a minority owner who was operating the company was not in favor of the sale.

We were proceeding with due diligence when we learned that this minority owner was attempting to secure financing and thwart the deal, in direct violation of the terms set forth in the Letter of Intent.

This created a significant issue with the majority owners, as well as considerable delays in closing the deal.

Lesson: Once the Letter of Intent is signed all parties must abide by its terms. Be sure minority owners are on board before signing the LOI.

business.

In addition to this basic list you should review the "EXEMPLAR OF REQUEST FOR DUE DILIGENCE DOCUMENTS" located at the end of this chapter, and begin to assemble any additional applicable documents. Since every business is unique and each industry has specific nuances, there may be additional disclosure items you are aware of that should be made known to a prospective buyer. Be sure to disclose those items even if they are not specifically requested.

Please believe us, while it may take some time to review and assemble these documents, you will see it was well worth it when your production of due diligence documentation is a breeze!

Some final thoughts on due diligence:

- Do not haggle the buyer to finalize the deal or hound them on how much longer due diligence will take. Every time we got pressure from the seller, we slowed down the process. Partly to show who was in control, but mainly to see if he or she was overly anxious and trying to rush the process because an upcoming issue was about to be exposed.

- Be open and honest! Withholding information that is later uncovered is potentially fraudulent and will come back to hurt you. If there are company secrets that should not be disclosed until after closing, such as a secret formula or software code, be sure the prospective buyer knows you will be providing full disclosure upon closing.

- During and following the due diligence process you will probably find yourself in continuing negotiations with the buyer. Recognize that you will not win every negotiation. As much as possible, put your ego on the shelf and take the emotion out of the equation. Sometimes buyers will realize during due diligence that a seller is in a desperate situation and look to take advantage of him.

  From time to time you may need to re-evaluate your reasons for selling and what the deal breakers are. . If you really feel the deal evolves into one that is not good for you, do not be afraid to walk away. If you choose to sever the deal, be prepared for the potential consequences of doing so, including the possibility of a breakup fee.

- Remember that following the signing of the LOI, there will be certain limitations placed upon you that may interfere with how you normally operate the company. No matter how frustrating it is, be sure to abide by any such restrictive terms or discuss any issues that may arise with the prospective buyer.

- As exasperating as it may be, remember that the timing of the process is usually in the buyer's purview. Even if you are well prepared, do everything right and present your documents in a complete and timely fashion, the deal will not close until the buyer is ready to do so.

- The Bottom Line - Being prepared for due diligence will hasten the process and almost always allow the closing to take place in a shorter time frame.

So, now it is time to begin getting prepared for due diligence. While it may be premature for you to put all your documentation together and get completely geared up at this time, every measure you take to review and organize your documentation now will be a tremendous benefit in the long run!

Keep in mind that the "Exemplar of Request For

Due Diligence Documents" located at the end of this chapter is a very exhaustive list. Do not be alarmed! Chances are you will not receive a request this broad in scope, and even if you do, most likely not all items on the list will be applicable.

Review Your Contracts and Agreements

Review every line of every contract and agreement to ensure there are no contractual obligations that could impact selling your business.

We recommend creating a chart listing each individual agreement by applicable category, such as shown below, with columns including expiration date, whether or not it is assignable, sections you may need to discuss with your legal counsel and other comments related to its impact on a sale of the business.

Agreement	Exp. Date	Assign-able?	Sections to discuss	Misc.
Employment Agreements				
Consulting Agreements				
Vendor Agreements				
Customer Agreements				
Distributor Agreements				
Retainer Agreements				
Licensing Agreements for patents, trademarks or other intellectual property				
Confidentiality/Non-compete Agreements				
Joint Venture, Partnership or Joint Development				
Loan Agreements				
Stock Sale Agreements				
Leases – Real estate, equipment, vehicle				
Letters of Intent				
Other miscellaneous agreements and contracts, governmental permits, approvals and licenses				

Memorandum

To:

From:

Date:

Subject: Due Diligence Review

Below is a list of documents and other information we would like to review in connection with the proposed acquisition of your company. This is a comprehensive list that is overly-broad due to our lack of familiarity with your company.

At your earliest convenience, please forward the documents requested that are applicable to your business. If there are some documents that are too voluminous to copy, we ask that you make them available for review at your place of business.

Please note that as our review proceeds, we may request additional items. If you have any questions please do not hesitate to contact us.

A. **Basic Corporate Documentation**
   a. Organizational documents including certificate or articles of incorporation and any amendments
   b. Bylaws of the Company
   c. Minutes of all meetings and written consents/resolutions of directors, committees of directors and stockholders
   d. List of all jurisdictions where property is owned or leased or where business is conducted
   e. Most recently obtained good standing certificates for all states and jurisdictions in which the Company is authorized to do business
   f. Business plans, both current and past
   g. Organizational chart showing all divisions, business units, subsidiaries and other affiliates
   h. Copies of any other organizational related documents

B. **Basic Corporate Documentation of Subsidiaries and Affiliates** – Provide a description of each along with the items listed above as it relates to each subsidiary, division or affiliate

C. **Capitalization**
   a. Schedules/Ledgers for each class of stock and other securities issued by the Company
   b. Copies of any voting trust, stockholder or other agreements related to the Company's securities
   c. All material information or documents given to directors or shareholders over the past two years.
   d. List of all outstanding options, including names and addresses of option holders, number of options, exercise price and vesting schedule
   e. Copies of stock option plans and forms of option agreements
   f. Copies of any stock purchase agreements that have been used for sales of the Company's stock.

g. Any other agreements and documents relating to sales of securities by the Company, including buy/sell agreements, right of first refusal or other offering circulars, escrow agreements and vesting agreements.

h. Evidence of qualification or exemption under state or federal securities laws for all issuances or transfers of Company's securities.

i. Any proxy and other information statements.

j. All offering documents used for equity and/or debt financing

k. Copies of any other contracts, arrangements, documentation or commitments relating to the stock of the Company

D. Material Contracts and Agreements

a. Description of key vendors, especially sole-source suppliers and copies of contracts, blanket purchase orders or significant purchase orders

b. Description of any customers representing more than 10% of the company's revenue, and copies of any customer related contracts or other significant agreements

c. Any agreements related to the acquisition or disposition of significant assets

d. Any joint venture, strategic alliance, distributorship, consulting and partnership agreements

e. All indemnification agreements, warranties, guarantees related to the company and/or its products

f. Any confidentiality, non-compete, non-solicitation and non-disclosure agreements

g. Agreements and documents related to loans to or from the Company along with any related payment schedules

h. Schedule of and copies of agreements related to exclusive rights granted by the Company to third parties

      i.   A schedule and copies of all consulting and other agreements regarding inventions, technology sharing, joint development and licenses or assignments of any intellectual property to or from the Company

      j.   Copies of leases for vehicles, equipment and furniture

      k.   Copies of all insurance policies and a schedule of any outstanding claims

      l.   Any documents related to any transactions or agreements with directors, officers or other stockholdings owning 5% or more of the Company

      m. Copies of other material documents, agreements, contract or leases related to the business and/or financial condition of the company not previously listed

E.   **Company Information and Literature**

      a.   Schedule of major competitors

      b.   Copies of articles and press releases issued by or relating to the Company within the past two years

      c.   Description of current products or services, anticipated new or enhanced products or services with comparative analysis with competitive product or services

      d.   Copies of brochures, flyers, sell sheets and other documents related to the Company and/or its products or services

      e.   Copies of reports or analyses prepared by third parties regarding the Company, its subsidiaries or products

      f.   Description of both the domestic and foreign industry including size, trends, pricing strategies and any other issues affecting industry growth and/or growth of the Company within the industry

      g.   Description of Company's pricing policies and strategies

F.   **Real Estate**

      a.   Schedule of all real property owned by the Company

    b.   Copies of title reports, appraisals and surveys or any real estate owned by the Company

    c.   Copies of deeds, variances, easements, restriction and any encumbrances in relation to real estate owned by the Company

    d.   Description of any environmental impact issues related to any property owned by the Company

    e.   Lease agreements for any real property owned by the Company

    f.   Lease agreements for all Company offices, warehouses or other facilities and any amendments

G.   **Patents**

    a.   Schedule of all foreign and domestic patents and any pending applications including the status of each

    b.   Copies of all patents, all pending and abandoned applications and all correspondence with the patent office

    c.   Copies of all invention disclosures

    d.   Schedule and copies of all licenses, assignments, technology transfer, distribution or consulting agreements and any other documents related to rights in or to the Company's patents

    e.   Description of any searches or investigations for potential patents or potential patent infringement for any of the Company's products

    f.   Proof of payments of patent maintenance fees

    g.   Schedule and description of any patents issued, applied for or contemplated that are owned by any officer, director or key employee that arose during the inventor's term as a key employee, officer or director of the Company

    h.   Copies of any documentation related to any claims or threatened claims by or against the Company as it relates to patents.

H. Copyrights, Trademarks, Trade Names and Internet Domains

a. Schedule of all foreign and domestic trademarks, trade names, copyrights and any pending applications, including current status of each

b. Schedule of all domain names used by the Company including expiration dates, hosting companies and related agreements

c. Schedule and copies of any unregistered copyrights, trade names and trademarks used by the Company, including the first date of use

d. Copies of opinions from legal counsel related to the Company's trademarks, trade names and copyrights

e. Schedule and copies of all licenses, rights, assignments, transfer or any other documents related to the rights in or to the Company's trademarks, trade names and copyrights

f. Copies of any other documents related to the Company's trademarks, trade names and copyrights including but not limited to cease and desist letters or other challenges

I. Other Proprietary Rights and Documents

a. Schedule of any proprietary information owned by or licensed to the Company that is not protected by patented, copyright, trademark or trade name, including processes, trade secrets or other confidential information related to the Company's products, services or business operations

b. Copies of any documentation valuing the Company's intellectual property or property rights

c. Copies of Company policies for protecting intellectual property, trade secrets and other proprietary information

J. Litigation

a. Schedule describing current, pending or threatened litigation, injunctions, disputes, governmental investigations or inquiries against the Company or its subsidiaries

    b.   Copies of all documents related to above

    c.   Schedule of recently settled litigation and copies of settlement agreements, decrees, order or judgments

    d.   Copies of correspondence with legal counsel regarding current, pending or threatened litigation, disputes, governmental investigations or inquiries

    e.   Copies of correspondence with auditors related to threatened or pending litigation, assessments or claims

K.   **Directors, Officers and Employees**

    a.   List of all directors and officers of the Company including bios and compensation for each

    b.   Copies of director and officer questionnaires

    c.   Description of any affiliation any director of officer may have with any government entity

    d.   Copies of all agreements with directors, officers and employees including but not limited to indemnification agreements, employment agreements, retirement agreements and plans, benefits agreements and plans, bonus plans, profit sharing plans, proprietary information and invention agreements, confidentiality agreements and non-competition agreements

    e.   Copies of collective bargaining agreement, if any and description of any significant labor issues

    f.   List of key employees, including position, compensation, years of service and relevant experience

    g.   Schedule indicating the number of employees by division, department and function and location

    h.   Management organizational chart

    i.   Copy of Company policy and procedure manual and employee handbook

L. **Financial and Operations**

    a. Copies of all correspondence with auditors related to internal accounting controls since inception

    b. Copies of most recent financial statements

    c. Copies of audited annual financial statements for the past three years

    d. Copies of all reports and correspondence with auditors for the past three years

    e. Copies of three most recent years of filed tax returns

    f. Copies of any reports or studies related to the Company's financial condition or valuation over the past three years

    g. List of banks or other lenders with whom the Company has a financial relationship

    h. Copy of the Company's general ledger

    i. Schedule of all indebtedness and contingent liabilities

    j. Schedule of tax liabilities

    k. Schedules of inventories

    l. Aging schedule of accounts receivable

    m. Aging schedule of accounts payable

    n. Schedule of fixed assets

    o. Analysis of gross margins

    p. Schedule of any off-balance sheet assets and liabilities

    q. Operating budget of the Company for the past three years

    r. Breakdown by account of all expenses classified as G&A, R&D and Cost of Revenues

    s. Breakdown of sales and gross profit by product, sales channel and geography

    t. Current backlog

    u. Copy of current and past business plans, including projections, capital

M. **Regulatory Issues**

    a. Copies of all domestic and foreign regulatory permits, licenses, approvals and entitlements for current and future projects and/or services for the Company and its subsidiaries

    b. Schedule of inspection history related to any permits, licenses, approvals or entitlements including the date, type of inspections, regulatory body and status of inspection issues

    c. Copies of inspection reports

    d. Copies of all correspondence with regulatory bodies

N. **Insurance**

    a. Schedule of the Company's insurance policies including but not limited to health, general liability, personal and real property, product liability, errors and omissions, key man, director's and officer's, worker's compensation and disability

    b. Copies of insurance policies

    c. Copies of any documentation related to any claims in relation to above policies

O. **Miscellaneous**

    a. Description of any Securities Act violations of the Company or any of its officers or directors

    b. Description of any criminal acts for which the Company or any of its officers or directors have been convicted

    c. Copies of any other documents, schedules or information that could reasonably impact the current or future valuation of the Company

16

PREPARING TO MEET
PROSPECTIVE BUYERS

Your initial meeting with a prospective buyer –
whether on the telephone or in person - is perhaps the
most important and significant step in the sales process.
Although by now they may have reviewed your
business profile and other information you may have
sent, it is not until they speak with you that they can get
a feel for the personality of both you and your business.
And you for them!

We recommend that you try to find out as much as
you can about the prospective buyer before engaging in

Zip the Lip

We met with the owner of a manufacturing company who was gregarious, very engaging and intimately involved with both his company and the industry.

Upon meeting, we all "clicked" and were very excited about doing a potential deal in which he would continue to be heavily involved in operations.

In subsequent telephone conversations, he became very relaxed and starting sharing stories – many quite funny – that made us realize he had potential drinking and gambling habits which we felt could possibly affect his role going forward. We opted not to pursue the deal.

Lesson: Don't let your guard down. Do not think of the prospective buyer as your buddy. Everything you say is being weighed and potentially judged.

meaningful conversation. We have been amazed at the amount of information some business owners have given us without even knowing our names!

An Internet search is a great place to start. But remember to keep in mind that information on the web can be inaccurate and misleading!

Some business consultants recommend that in the initial conversations you "interview" the potential buyers to find out what their goals are and the return they are looking to get through the purchase of your company. They also encourage sellers to ascertain whether or not the person has the financial ability to buy your company. That strategy might work well for some, but from our personal perspective, if we were looking to give our money to someone, the last thing we would tolerate is an inquisition.

Yes, you certainly want to engage the buyer in conversation, and learn something that will allow you to tailor your pitch or sense if the person is "for real" – but if you ask too many questions, come on too aggressively or make them feel like they're being interrogated, it will most likely backfire on you.

It is important that you be prepared for the conversation with prospective buyers. First of all, before commencing any detailed discussion, be sure you have a signed confidentiality agreement. It is usually very difficult to engage in a conversation with a prospective buyer without revealing confidential information. Following any discussion, when applicable, remember to follow up with a written statement that the information you shared with them is covered under the terms of the confidentiality agreement.

Often the very first question that will be asked of you is, "Why are you selling?" Your answer will set the tone of the entire process with him/her. From your response they will gauge just how desperate you are to sell – no matter what your reasons are - and how much they may be able to take advantage of your situation for their benefit.

However desperate you may be, you can provide an answer that will perhaps make them see an acquisition of your company as a challenge they would want to take on. For example, if you have to sell – whether it is because you cannot afford to stay in business, are getting divorced or battling an illness, you can either tell that to the buyer (not a good idea) or you can simply say, "I recognize that I'm not the person that can take this company to the next level." Now you've set the stage for that prospective buyer to decide if he or she is that qualified person. Their ego will almost always tell them they are!

The next question you need to be prepared for is, "Why should I buy your company?" Once again, your answer is critical.

We recommend being prepared by developing an "elevator pitch" response for these questions. The more you know about the prospective buyer, including why he or she is interested in acquiring your business, the better you can tailor your reply. The buyer is not looking for a long drawn out answer. He's looking for a succinct response, but will usually follow it up with a myriad of questions.

In your discussions, expect to answer a lot of questions. Previously it was mentioned that buyers do not want to be interrogated, but in essence, that is what they will be doing to you. At the end of this chapter is a list of generic questions you may be asked, whether in the first meeting or during due diligence. You should be prepared to answer these, as well as questions more specific to your company and related to the documentation you provide.

Do not be offended by or get annoyed with someone who asks a lot of questions, particularly the ones that come across as a cross-examiner. Those are often the ones that are the most serious potential buyers!

Expect the prospect to ask questions related to information you already sent with a heavy emphasis on financial related issues. Even if the prospective buyer is viewing your business as a strategic acquisition, the financial condition both historically and currently, is still very important for him or her to understand.

Be prepared to answer inquiries concerning recurring revenues and trends in revenue and profits. Unless your revenue chart looks like the proverbial "hockey stick curve" indicating sustained growth year after year, a buyer will certainly have questions.

It may be that your revenue chart looks more like a mountain range with significant peaks and valleys, or it might depict such a sharp decline that it looks like your company has fallen off a cliff.

If so, be prepared to explain to a buyer what was happening in your business or industry that affected revenues. And be honest. A potential buyer may know a lot more than you realize, and you could look like a fool if you attempt to cover up an inadequacy with an untruthful excuse.

Perhaps your best sales person left or you weren't hands-on in a down year. Remember, if you were less involved because you were ill, you do not necessarily need to be that specific. (Keep in mind however, that there may be times that disclosure of an illness would be necessary or even advantageous. Only you can determine that.)

Or, perhaps the entire industry was affected by the economy. If that's the case, be prepared to explain why your business will not stay that way and the steps you took to insulate your business from future economic stress. If in a down market you out-performed your competitors be sure to make that known. If your competitors went out of business during the recession, tout it. It will show you will have less competition going forward, and that you had the ability to weather the storm.

If your company's revenues and/or bottom line have been impacted by the recession you may want to show a pre-recession financial recap in addition to projections based upon where you expect the industry and your company to be in the future and why.

If the above-mentioned charts represented trends in your profits, you should also be prepared to discuss what affected your bottom line. Perhaps you had a significant write-off or spent more for advertising or employee training. Be sure to explain the benefits those expenses may have going forward. If poor management impacted profits, do not shy away from telling them. The buyer will *always* think he could have done a better job managing it!

If you have very low revenues because your company has been involved in research and development, or building the next Internet sensation, you will need to be prepared to explain why the company has value to be acquired now.

Some advisors encourage sellers to tell the prospective buyer that he/she has other suitors, theoretically to portray that they are in demand. If it is not true, do not do it. We have all experienced that type of selling before, as it is used frequently by real estate brokers to try to get you to make an offer on a house "before the people I showed it to this morning do".

If you do not really have someone else looking to buy your company, do not try to bluff the prospective acquirer. Unless this is their first acquisition, they have probably seen this tactic used before and will sometimes bluff you back and walk away, even if they really are interested. When you come crawling back ("Gee, the other deal fell through") two things have happened: (1) They've lost trust in you; (2) They now have a strong upper hand.

A few tips to consider when meeting with potential buyers:

- Be personable. A savvy and experienced buyer is not expecting every seller to be full of vibrant personality, but a level of enthusiasm for your business certainly engages the buyer to want to know more.

- Be honest. There is nothing more annoying to a buyer than to be told what he wants to hear, only to find out later that it is not true.

- Be positive. Even if not everything in the business is rosy, no prospective buyer wants to hear a sob story on why you had a bad last quarter. If there are negative issues to explain do so, but do not belabor the point, makes excuses, complain or point fingers.

- Be professional. When a seller does not come across as professional, buyers often will perceive it as a weakness and think they can take advantage of them. Be sure to portray that you know your business like the back of your hand as well as what is happening in the industry. And when meeting in person "dress for success"!

- Be focused. Respond with complete, but concise answers. Do not ramble or digress to off-topic issues. Often it is in those ramblings that buyers hear things they do not like.

- Be confident. Buyers like dealing with a confident – but not smug – seller. By being confident in yourself, your business and in the fact that you will be able to secure a buyer, the suitor will deduce that are not in a desperate situation.

So, now it is time to get prepared for your initial discussion with prospective buyers. Your first step is to prepare your "elevator pitches". The second is to anticipate the questions you could be asked by a potential buyer.

Develop Your Elevator Pitches

Imagine getting into an elevator and pressing the button to the tenth floor. A stranger in the elevator asks why you are selling your business, and you need to have a complete answer before you reach the tenth floor. You've got 30 seconds – a minute max.

That is your "elevator pitch". You can also think of it as a verbal Tweet – a succinct but complete response.

Remember that you do not necessarily need to divulge *all* the reasons you are selling. You may want to review chapter four, "Why Are You Selling?" before completing this task.

You should prepare an elevator pitch not only for why you are selling your business, but also for why someone should want to buy it. You may want to review chapter six, "Why Should Someone Buy Your Business?" before completing this task.

Depending on your audience, you may need to tweak your elevator pitch, and from time-to-time may need to update it.

You should audibly practice your elevator pitch and always be prepared to deliver it!

---

(1) Write your "elevator pitch" to answer, *"Why you are selling your company?"* If you are selling because you want to retire, be prepared for a follow up question of why you want to retire at this time.

_____

_____

_____

_____

_____

_____

_____

_____

_____

_____

_____

_____

_____

_____

_____

_____

_____

_____

_____

_____

_____

(2) Write your elevator pitch to answer, *"Why should I buy your company?"*   Be sure to include your differentiating factors and competitive advantages.

_____

_____

_____

_____

_____

_____

_____

_____

_____

_____

_____

_____

_____

_____

_____

_____

_____

_____

_____

_____

Anticipate Questions

Anticipate the **top five financial** related questions you will be asked *based on information you will have provided* to the prospective buyer, and how you would respond. (Use additional paper if necessary.)

1._____

_____

_____

_____

_____

_____

_____

2._____

_____

_____

_____

_____

_____

_____

_____

3.

4.

5.

Anticipate the **top five operational** related questions you will be asked, *based on information you will have provided* to them, and how you would respond. (Use additional paper if necessary.)

1._____

_____

_____

_____

_____

_____

_____

_____

2._____

_____

_____

_____

_____

_____

_____

_____

_____

3.

4.

5.

50 Common Questions to Anticipate

1. Why are you selling?

2. What are you selling?

3. When was the company founded?

4. How did you get into the business?

5. What is the company's history?

6. Who are your key employees, and what positions do they hold?

7. How many employees do you have by category?

8. How is your business organized? (S Corp, C Corp LLC etc.)

9. Where are you incorporated?

10. Where are you authorized to do business?

11. How many owners/partners and percentage of ownership of each?

12. What is the current year's revenue?

13. What was past 3 to 5 year revenue?

14. What is your primary product or service? (Or best selling, most profitable etc.)

15. What is your current geographic market? Is it expandable?

16. What is the size of the industry/market?

17. What percentage of that market do you have?

18. What is your estimated growth over the next

three to five years?

19. What are your average gross margins?

20. What products/services have the highest gross margin?

21. How does that compare to margins in the industry/market?

22. Are you cash flow positive?

23. What is the current book value of the company?

24. What is the current working capital?

25. What are the current receivables? Payables?

26. What is your current short-term debt position?

27. What is your current long-term debt position?

28. Are tax returns filed up to date?

29. Do you have any tax liabilities?

30. Do you have an in-house accountant?

31. What accounting software do you use?

32. How have you been funded/financed?

33. Has your company been audited?

34. What barriers to entry exist in your industry/market?

35. What is your product/service differentiation? (Price, function, etc.)

36. Does any customer represent more than 10% of your revenue?

37. How do you sell/distribute your product?

38. What government regulations are in effect that have a negative impact on your business? Any that are beneficial to the business?

39. Are there any pending regulations that will effect the company in any way?

40. Do you have any patents, trademarks, copyrights, licensing agreements or other intellectual property of value?

41. Are you reliant upon any other company's technology or intellectual property?

42. Do you have any sole source suppliers?

43. Do you have any current or pending lawsuits?

44. Do you have any material contracts with vendors, customers or joint venture partners?

45. Do you have a written business plan?

46. Are you out of compliance with any registrations, licenses, agreements etc.?

47. Do you have any employment agreements or collective bargaining agreements?

48. What is your employee turnover rate?

49. What is the greatest mistake or failure the company has had?

50. What other companies or businesses are you personally currently involved with? How about in the past?

17

PREPARING FOR A SITE VISIT

When a potential acquirer wants to meet and see your operation, once again, you need to be sure that the first impression is a good one. Think of it as if your prospective in-laws were coming to your house for dinner for the first time. You need to put your best foot forward.

If you were going on a job interview you would wear your finest appropriate clothes. If you were selling your product or services, your web site and marketing materials would be up to date and top notch. If you were selling your car, you would have it detailed and waxed. Likewise, if you want to sell your business

Over Staged

We commenced due diligence on a small manufacturing company that we knew was struggling, but we were interested in tapping into their distribution channel.

At the initial site visit, we toured the very neat facility and took note of the products we were told were going through the final quality control inspection before being shipped. The items were very neatly organized and laid out in a very precise manner.

Upon returning a for a second and third time over the course of a few weeks, we noted that the items were untouched and positioned exactly the same way as they had been on our first visit, clearly demonstrating there was even less going on than we were being led to believe.

Lesson: Have your facility neat and organized, but do not over-stage it for a site visit. It usually is very obvious and can make you look both untrustworthy and foolish.

you need to have a professional polished look.

You also need to be sure that during the visit, the prospective buyer sees consistency. If your website says or depicts one thing, and you are telling or showing the suitor something contradictory, it will raise a red flag.

As a side note, be sure your website is updated with your current products or services. Remove any links that do not work. If your press releases or Company News are not current, either update or remove irrelevant information. Verify that the copyright date at the bottom of each page includes the most current year, and that your contact information is correct.

Be sure that any forms or email contacts from your website are responded to in a timely fashion. If not, remove them. Many prospective buyers will look to get information about your company via this method before they ever contact you. Not getting a response will immediately give them a questionable view of how your company is run.

Since every business is unique, there will never be two identical site visits. Some initial site visits will take place before an offer is made and the Letter of Intent (LOI) signed. Others will take place after the signing of the LOI and at the commencement of due diligence.

Usually there will be multiple visits during the due diligence phase. You should know the purpose of each of these visits beforehand so you can best be prepared for them. In a few unique situations where it is critical that employees not be told about the acquisition until after closing, the site visit may not come until after the deal closes.

There are obvious ways that you should prepare for the prospective buyer's initial visit, such as having the offices be clean and neat. But there are other things you should consider, as well. Is the outside of the facility neat and clean? Is the landscaping trimmed and windows washed? Are the employees and their work areas professional looking? Does it look like you are busy – or going out of business? Sometimes being too neat or over-staged can also raise a red flag, as it may look like nothing is going on! ("A creative mess is better than tidy idleness!")

Take steps to ensure that the potential buyer will view your company as being up-to-date.

When visiting a potential acquisition, we would look at the bulletin board displaying employee postings and take note if it was outdated. In the conference room or showroom, we would ask questions about the

Obsolescence

Upon our initial meeting with an acquisition target, we were given a tour of the manufacturing facility.

At first glance, it looked impressive, with multiple projects appearing to be in various stages of fabrication in several areas throughout the facility. However, once we began asking some rudimentary questions, we received responses such as, "we used to make this" or "when so-and-so worked here we used this manufacturing area."

This made us research deeper into the obsolescence and therefore the value of the inventory, as well as the overall health of the company.

Lesson: Be sure your facility is current with where your company is today. Discard obsolete inventory from your manufacturing facility. Unless they are there to display a history of the company, be sure your showroom is up-to-date with outdated products removed.

products displayed and take note if they were obsolete. If something was out of place, or there was a large stack of papers in a corner, on our next visit, we would see if it was still that same way.

Without speaking to them, we observed the employees and noted how they interacted with each other. On subsequent visits, we would take note that the same people were there.

Do not go to the extreme of hiring temps to make the place look full (as is often done!) but when feasible, make sure all your employees are in-house with work to do. And note, they do not have to know who you are meeting with or why. Depending on the situation, if asked, you can say you are exploring ways to take the company to the next level.

During site visits, most buyers will have respect for you and your operations and not attempt to get in the way of your business. If you have not told your employees that you are looking to sell the business, be sure the prospective buyer is fully aware of your desire to be discrete about the sale.

All meetings should take place behind closed doors, in a room from which you are certain conversations cannot be overheard from an adjacent area. Depending on the situation, it may be best to provide a tour of your facility, and hold subsequent discussions off-site. Or, sometimes it might be best to hold the initial site visit after hours.

Sellers often wonder if they should have their legal counsel present for a site visit. A general rule of thumb is that if the buyer is bringing a lawyer, you should at a minimum have access to your counsel telephonically in case a legal issue arises. Generally, a buyer will not have his attorney accompany him unless the LOI has been signed and the due diligence process has begun.

If the initial site visit takes place prior to signing the LOI, it is best to keep the meeting short – an hour to an hour and a half. Remember that your job in this meeting is to sell them on your business, and provide enough information to get them to take it to the level of making an offer and signing an LOI. So try to stay focused!

During the visit, it is recommended that you remain physically close to the prospective buyer. An innocent visit to the restroom down the hall could give him or her access – intentionally or accidentally – to an area, person or activity that you may not want them to be exposed to yet.

If the LOI has been signed and the site visit is being conducted as a part of due diligence, the initial visit will probably be longer with more detailed information being shared. Depending on where you are in the process, you may have already given the prospective buyer the documentation you have prepared for due diligence. If so, this first meeting may include a review of those documents, with inquiries regarding various aspects of them.

If you have not previously given these documents to the buyer, you may wish to present them along with a verbal overview of what is included. The buyer will need time to review the documents after leaving your facility, and probably will not have a lot of questions about them until a subsequent conversation. Having your due diligence documents ready to give to the prospective buyer will help to keep the meeting focused.

It is also important to mention that a prospective buyer is not necessarily your friend! Often, sellers get a comfort factor with a potential acquirer and open up to him or her – telling far more than they need to about their personal life, or issues going on within the company or with a particular employee. You never know if something you mention innocently in a passing conversation could be a turn-off. A buyer is always looking to find a weakness that could give them an

Spin

A new start-up competitor was beginning to make some "noise" in our industry, so we put out an offer to buy them.

The owners had raised a considerable amount of private financing that was to be used for the development and manufacturing of expensive equipment needed to produce their product.

Upon touring the facility, we learned they had utilized a significant amount of their funds outfitting the offices for prospective future growth including several workstations complete with leased computers and other office equipment. (They had just two office employees!)

The sellers tried to spin their bad decision, touting that the company was positioned for growth. All we saw was the liability of empty workstations containing equipment that was becoming more obsolete by the day, while they were still trying to get their manufacturing equipment to work properly.

Lesson: You may not be able to change a bad decision or situation, but leave the spin to the politicians and do not try to pass it off as an advantage to a prospective buyer.

advantage during negotiations, or a heads up on due diligence. Do not fall into that trap!

It is also particularly recommend that you resist the offer from a buyer to go out for a drink. Buyers often use this relaxed atmosphere when your guard is down to find out more about you and the business – especially if they are considering having you to stay with the company. If you decide that it is in your best interest to accept an invitation, it is recommended that you order a soft drink. We have always been amazed at how much more people will talk after a just drink or two! And take note: The buyer, while encouraging you to have "one more" often is not imbibing!!

As best you can, be relaxed for your visits. A buyer will expect you may be a bit nervous, but if you appear to be too uptight, it could raise a red flag.

While the majority of what you will need to do to prepare for a site visit will come after you have found a prospective buyer, there are some things you can do now to prepare your facility and then keep updated as you go along. Doing certain things now may also help make a pending sale down the road less noticeable to your employees.

So, let's get you prepared for a site visit!

Website

Review your website and list changes that need to be made now to bring it up to date and/or to be consistent with what a potential buyer would see at your facility today.

_____

_____

_____

_____

_____

_____

_____

_____

_____

_____

_____

_____

_____

_____

_____

_____

_____

What website items should you review/update on a regular basis?

_____

_____

_____

_____

_____

_____

_____

_____

_____

_____

_____

_____

_____

_____

_____

_____

_____

_____

Facility

Prior to a site visit from a potential buyer, make a checklist of all you will need to do to prepare for the visit, including copying of any documents you may need to present. Be sure all tasks are completed before the visit!

Here are some items to consider:

(1) Be sure your facility is clean. Have the windows washed, carpets cleaned and linoleum waxed. Fix broken fixtures and equipment and replace burned-out bulbs.

(2) Inventory. Create a list of raw material inventory that has not been used, or finished goods inventory that has not been sold in the past two years. Unless there is good reason to believe these items will be used or sold in the near future, consider disposing of them. (You should discuss with your accountant how such inventory should be accounted for.)

(3) Showroom. Inspect your showroom or other areas in which you display your products or services. Remove any items that are not relevant to what your company is today, unless they are fitting for portraying the history of the company.

(4) Bulletin boards. Review the items on your employee bulletin boards to verify that all information posted is up to date and accurate. Be sure to recheck it from time to time, and specifically just prior to a site visit.

(5) Work areas. Encourage employees to work neatly. Remove any items from work areas that are not utilized and if necessary, purchase items to aid in organization of tools or document usage and storage.

(6) Inspections. If your business requires that your facility be inspected from time to time (i.e.: Health Department; FDA; ISO; EPA; etc) be sure you are in complete compliance to pass any such inspection at all times. Be prepared to discuss any prior issues that may have resulted from such inspections and what was done to correct the issue.

18

RING THE BELL?

For many business owners, the ultimate purchaser of their business would be the "public", achieved through the selling of shares of the company's stock in an initial public offering (IPO).

Depending on the valuation of a company and/or its future prospects, going public could actually be the best way to effectuate an exit strategy.

Going public can be a significant undertaking, not to mention the steep cost. There are many things to consider with respect to taking a company public and a number of pros and cons:

- **PROS**
  - Raising capital in a public company is almost always easier than raising money in a private company. When stock has a publicly quoted price, it provides a benchmark from which to raise capital in both private and public offerings. Investors generally prefer to invest in publicly traded companies due to the liquidity of the stock, as well as the timely and transparent financial reporting requirements.
  - By virtue of being a publicly traded company, provided that a market exits for the stock, shareholders have the comfort of knowing they can sell out of their positions whenever they want, with limited restrictions. Liquidity is one of the reasons public companies are typically valued higher than private businesses.
  - Once a company is public and the market for its stock is established, the company has the benefit of being able to use its publicly traded status to grow its business through mergers and acquisitions. The

public valuation almost always provides a substantial advantage when exchanging shares in an acquisition, or when using the stock as currency in an asset purchase.

Additionally, a public company with an established public market valuation and having current disclosure statements filed with the Securities and Exchange Commission (SEC) is traditionally a more viable acquisition target.

o Converting a private entity to a public company generally results in a sizeable increase in the value of the business. If two companies with the same basic structure and financial position are operating within the same industry, the publicly traded corporation will by and large have a considerably higher market value than the private business.

o In both private and public companies, stock compensation can be used as an incentive to attract and retain key employees. It is also a way of connecting an employee's financial future to the company's success. These rewards, whether issued in the form of stock options or grants of common stock, are far more desirable when the company is publicly traded, allowing public companies to potentially hire better qualified employees.

o Most private companies are invisible not only to potential investors, but also to potential business partners for which synergistic opportunities may exist. As a rule, public companies receive a greater level of exposure to media outlets, allowing the company's story to be shared with a wider audience.

The investor relations strategies employed by public companies commonly have a cross-over effect for public relations, leading to increased awareness through various media channels both within and outside the company's industry. Such news stories can potentially attract the awareness of both investors and strategic business opportunities.

o The status of being a public company can have a dramatic effect on a company's image, as it creates a perception of prestige and greater stability. This perception can lead to expanded business opportunities and confidence from investors, customers, vendors and employees.

o For founders, a primary benefit of achieving public status is that their holdings of the company's stock are more liquid providing the opportunity for diversification of assets, potentially increasing personal net worth and offering greater financial stability and independence. Public company status can be used as a part of estate planning for founders, particularly when their heirs are not involved in the business.

Additionally, executive management of publicly traded companies is customarily compensated at a higher level.

- **CONS**

o The costs associated with going public are significant and the time executive management needs to expend in the effort is demanding, which could potentially impact the operations of the business.

After dedicating time and resources to the process, even with a firm underwriting agreement there is no guarantee that a company will achieve public trading status.

o In addition to the initial costs related to getting public, operating a public company increases overhead due in part to the required reporting and compliance issues. Additionally, the expanded responsibilities of executive management generally requires the hiring of separate operating management. These ongoing costs must be weighed against the benefits of being public in order to ascertain if they are worth it.

o For the benefit of shareholders, public companies are required to make periodic disclosure filings with the SEC. This includes an Annual Report with audited financial statements and a proxy statement, as well as quarterly update reports. Additionally, disclosure filings and press releases are required to be issued whenever there are events that could have potential impact on the company's stock price, whether positively or negatively. Competent personnel must be hired to ensure these and other reporting requirements are met in a timely fashion.

- By virtue of being public, it is far easier for the general public, including competitors, to be able to see what might otherwise be considered proprietary information. In addition to financial results, the company must disclose certain business strategies and executive management compensation packages and stockholdings.

- Public companies are held to a higher operating standard. They are governed by regulatory issues that require the Chief Executive Officer and Chief Financial Officer to personally certify to the effectiveness of the company's internal controls related to financial reporting, in addition to disclosure controls and procedures. The Board of Directors, management and all employees are required to adhere to the company's strict publicly published Code of Ethics.

- Taking a company public will result in the

dilution of the percentage of ownership of the founders, and may eventually lead to founders no longer owning a controlling interest in the company. In the event the company under performs, a group of dissident shareholders may vote to replace the board of directors and demand a change of management.

o   After taking a company public, executive management in essence works for the shareholders. Decisions must not only be weighed in accordance with what is best for the company's future growth, but also in accordance with the wishes of current shareholders, which are often more aligned with short-term goals.

o   Although most shareholders rarely if ever contact the company, it is not unusual for investors to reach out to management when there has been a significant change in the price or trading volume of the stock, or when a press release has been issued. In light of disclosure regulations, responding to the demands of shareholders can be stressful. Public companies must hire an investor relations firm or have competent personnel appointed to handle investors' concerns ,who are familiar with both the regulatory issues and the company's operations.

There are multiple ways a company can achieve public trading status. Options include:

- **Underwritten Initial Public Offering (IPO)**
An underwritten IPO is the method of going public with which people are most familiar. In this process one or more brokerage firms *underwrite* the offering. The firm or firms purchase the company's shares from the issuer and then sell those shares to their clients. A "hot" IPO will have high investor appeal and demand, often sending the opening price of the stock surging.

The IPO market can be fickle. A given industry category can be favorable one year with many deals being completed even on lower-tier companies, and the next year a top-rated company in that industry with great credentials is unable to find an underwriter who will return a call.

For small businesses, the underwritten IPO process has always been tenuous. As regulatory requirements for underwriters have become more stringent in recent years, smaller brokerage firms have been forced out of business making it increasingly difficult for small companies to obtain an underwriter, with the exception of certain high tech or research companies.

Even if a small business is fortunate enough to secure a firm commitment from an underwriter, a shift in market conditions or issues within the industry or company can allow the underwriter to negate the deal, and the company will lose both the time and money invested in the process.

- **Self-Underwritten Offering** Because of the dearth of underwriters available for micro-cap offerings, small businesses may consider a self-written underwriting. Typically, this is a difficult process because most business owners do not have direct access to potential investors. Furthermore, they must create a market for the trading of the stock while being certain to not run afoul of ever-changing rigorous regulations.

• **Reverse Merger** A reverse merger, also known as "backing into a shell" occurs when a private company merges with a public shell (a public entity without operations) and emerges as the controlling operating public company. In recent years, many small businesses have used this method in order to achieve public trading status, but there are many risks and downsides to doing so. The cost can be extensive; lack of proper due diligence can produce adverse results; due to stigma many investors will not even consider purchasing the stock; and, the SEC so highly scrutinizes such transactions, that the company may never be able to satisfy the demands of the agency.

• **Form 10 Registration** A lesser known alternative method for obtaining public status is the filing of a Form 10 registration statement with the SEC. With this option, the company can not simultaneously raise money (which is usually the reason for going public) and the company must qualify in order to meet certain regulatory issues.

This method of going public is typically used by an already publicly traded company that is spinning off a division or subsidiary.

Although not every company is suitable to be publicly traded, be careful not to be easily dissuaded by naysayers who may tell you your business can not go public. If you are serious about the possibility of doing so, investigate the potential opportunity with tenacity. From our personal experience of being five-for-five in taking companies public – four underwritten IPOs and one Form 10 spin-off - we can attest to the fact that you can go public even if your company does not meet all the criteria being espoused by large Wall Street institutions.

Ringing the opening bell on the trading floor of the stock exchange following the IPO of one of our companies was a memorable experience. If you are considering taking your company public, it could be a great experience for you, as well. But you must be certain to take the issues discussed in this chapter into consideration. And remember, it is imperative that you engage the services of expert legal and accounting professionals with extensive experience in securities law and the requisite regulatory issues.

19

FINAL THOUGHTS

In conclusion, getting prepared to sell your business can be time consuming, and for some, a costly endeavor. But not being prepared will ultimately turn out to be *more time consuming* and often a *more costly* endeavor. Not to mention more stressful!

No matter how well prepared you may be, it is important to recognize that your business might not sell.

There could be numerous reasons for this, many of which may be completely out of your control, such as a bad economy or new government regulations that impact your industry or business. The reality is, many small businesses just do not sell. If you have done everything right and you are unable to sell your business, you do have some options.

Depending on why you are selling, the size and type of your business and the industry in which it operates, you may want to consider these alternatives:

- Liquidate assets. In some situations, "the sum of the parts is worth more than the whole". If you have saleable assets such as real estate, current inventory, a great domain name, an extensive email list, valuable equipment, desirable patent or trademark or even your phone number, you can parcel them off to various buyers and perhaps net more money than you would by selling all the assets or the stock of the company to one entity. This can be time consuming, but may be well worth the effort.

- Bring on a partner. It is not unusual for an entrepreneur to grow weary of working alone. Bringing on a new partner with fresh ideas can reenergize the business, and potentially increase its value. It may also furnish you with a buyer for the business down the road

Beware, however, that bringing on a partner will change the dynamics of your business and could introduce a whole new set of issues. We acquired three companies in which we bought out partners who were seemingly the best of friends. In every situation they viciously turned on each other shortly after the closing.

We trust you have gained valuable insight through the reading of this book. and that you are now better prepared to sell your business!

If you have not yet completed the tasks included, we recommend that you go back and do so. It is through these tasks that you will be able to determine, *if* you really want to sell your business, *why* you want to sell your business, *what* you need to do to prepare to sell it, *how* to effectuate a sale, *what* you will do afterwards – and so much more!

Want to sell your business? Get prepared!

MEET THE AUTHORS

James Witham and Karen Laustsen have acquired numerous businesses and are well versed in and have a unique perspective of what a buyer needs to see in order to move forward with an acquisition.

They know what buyers are looking for and looking at, and the things that drive them away. This insight allows them to assist owners in getting prepared to sell their business.

They have acquired companies involved in research and development, product development, product licensing, importing, manufacturing and distribution across a broad spectrum of industries, including:

- Alternative energy
- Municipal, industrial and commercial water treatment
- Residential water treatment
- Tire recycling
- Alcohol breath testing products
- Drug testing technology
- Information technology
- Sporting goods
- Toys

James Witham

Over a 20 year span, Jim Witham served as Chairman and Chief Executive Officer of five companies he founded and took public through firm-commitment investment banker underwritten offerings that traded on the American Stock Exchange or the OTCBB. The growth of these companies was facilitated largely through acquisitions.

One of these companies, which year-after-year was one of the most active trading stocks on the American Stock Exchange, was included for two consecutive years in the top 100 of *Inc.* magazine's list of *Fastest Growing Small Public Companies,* as well as in the top 150 of the nation's fastest growing technology companies in the *National Technology Fast 500 Program.*

Mr. Witham is a recipient of the prestigious *Ellis Island Medal of Honor*, which has been bestowed to a handful of Americans including six US Presidents, Supreme Court Justices, other politicians and dignitaries, entertainers, sports figures and business leaders across the nation.

Along with Donald Trump, Lee Iacocca, George Steinbrenner and other well-known business leaders Mr. Witham sat on the executive committee of the All

American Collegiate Golf Foundation, founded by Arnold Palmer, and received the "Humanitarian of the Year" award from that organization.

Mr. Witham has worked closely with Fortune 500 companies in addition to investment bankers and top investor relations and public relations firms. His extensive contact list includes CEOs of major US corporations and well-known media and sports personalities.

Mr. Witham is an avid sports fan and enjoys playing golf and engaging in other outdoor activities.

Karen Laustsen

After obtaining a degree in education, Karen Laustsen exchanged the classroom for the boardroom. She has served in executive positions and on the boards of directors of five publicly traded companies.

Ms. Laustsen has extensive experience in conducting due diligence on acquisition targets across a broad spectrum of industry sectors and sizes of companies. Other corporate responsibilities have included corporate governance, compliance, investor relations and public relations.

As a recipient of the gift sight through corneal transplants, Ms. Laustsen is an ardent advocate of eye, organ and tissue donation and supports guidedog programs for the blind and visually impaired.

The authors provide consulting services to small business owners that are considering selling their business, as well as to the buyers who are seeking to acquire them. For more information, please visit www.PutItTogether.BIZ or call 800-514-1407.

www.ingramcontent.com/pod-product-compliance
Lightning Source LLC
Chambersburg PA
CBHW071415180526
45170CB00001B/111